The Freedom to Love

~ The Life and Vision of Catherine Harding ~

Karin Visser

NSP

United Kingdom

THE FREEDOM TO LOVE

Second English edition published May 2019 by New Sarum Press

Layout and design: Julian Noyce

ISBN:978-1-9993535-5-1

NSP

New sarum Press | 6 Folkestone Road | Salisbury | SP2 8JP
United Kingdom

'My role is to send love around me to all the people here,
to all people around the world,
to my children, to anyone I encounter.
The only thing that counts is love:
that is my conclusion at the end of my life.

'I have always thought this,
but now I live it.
I really see that this is the only thing
that has results for the people I meet and live with.

'The best thing I can do
is to care for other people
and to constantly see
that I am them.'

Catherine Harding

Contents

Prologue

The air is hot at the little French airport, compared to the cool Dutch spring I've arrived from. Catherine had already warned me not to wait outside in the burning sun but to stay inside the airport hall. I have been sitting here for over half an hour now, worrying that I might not recognise her in the crowd. Did I give her the right time for my arrival?

What am I doing here? Where did this strange idea come from to interview her about her life? I hardly know her. Neither she nor I have ever done anything like this before. But my impulse to do this had stood out clearly against any feeling of personal uneasiness.

After our first meeting I had gathered my courage and written an email requesting an interview, which she never answered. I'd felt discouraged but the impulse remained. Later I'd heard through a friend that she was not well and was recovering from a hip operation, much more slowly than she had expected. I wrote a second email to which again she didn't reply. I then heard she'd had another setback due to a car accident. My third email, months later, she did answer, sweetly, with many apologies and a warm welcome to come to her apartment in Montpellier in the south of France.

I get up from the airport chair, and while I walk around to stretch my legs, I try to spot her face in the hustle and bustle around me. And I think of how we met in Salisbury at the yearly gathering of the Headless Way, a tradition put in place by Douglas Harding, her late husband.

Of course I'd already known her name and face from pictures, but meeting her in person had been a surprise to me. She was a strikingly radiant lady, in her eighties, full of energy and open to everyone, whether they were old friends or new to the Headless scene. A few days later she suggested we have lunch together, to which I happily agreed.

During the lunch she proved to be a good storyteller and shared a few events from her own life: she was the mother of five children; she had been a working single mother for many years; and she'd been married twice. Her story spoke to my own personal story.

I kept noticing that, as well as being a fellow female, a mother and a wise elder, she was such a bright being. To me she was an inspiration that it is possible to live your life in accordance with reality, if you see and acknowledge who you truly are and make your choices accordingly.

The idea of recording her stories and her vision had probably already arisen then, but only when I was back at home did the impulse begin to knock on my door insistently.

So that is why I am waiting here in the French heat, despite the fact that my feelings of uncertainty are increasing by the minute.

Finally I see her coming, on the arm of a young man who must be one of her sons. I recognise her immediately, of course: she shines. Her welcome is warm. She apologises for being late. Then we go off to her home and into an adventure that would soon grow into a dear friendship.

As sisters in Seeing, she said.

Karin Visser

Few things are truly important in life, especially not money. But what is important is love. 'We must love each other,' my father used to say. This is the only education I really got.

1
Love and the big disillusionment

The next morning we sit at Catherine's kitchen table in her apartment. The building in which she lives is brand new. Her furniture also is new: colourful, modern but not expensive. Everything about her home indicates that this is a new beginning. We make tea and find out that we both like it the English way: black, strong and with milk. She breaks up a bar of chocolate. 'Comfort food,' she laughs. 'I love chocolate!' We talk for a while, then I ask her how we should start. Without hesitation she says: 'I think the best way to start is from scratch!'

Of course! I can't help but smile and I turn on my recorder. When she begins to speak her tone is cheerful. She laughs a lot. In addition to the many difficulties and hardships, her life has been full of fascinating and amusing events.

I was born on April 16th 1932 at five o'clock in the morning. That is what they tell me, although I must confess I don't remember anything of it. My father was a professor, a physicist. He did research at the University of Strasbourg. My mother was a lovely lady. My sister was twelve years older than me and my mother couldn't get pregnant again after she was born. They didn't know why at the time. However, she had a condition which is now known to be very common. When they found the reason, she was operated on, and then she had my brother and me. When I was born my mother was 42 years old. This must be why I'm a little crazy! It's old for a woman to give birth.

We lived in Strasbourg, in Alsace, and we were a happy family although we had little money. Professors or teachers in France were not given big salaries. My father said, 'Never mind! Money is not important; the only important thing is love.' Those words have followed me my whole life.

The war broke out in September 1939. I was seven and a half years old. My memories from before the war are very sweet. I know that I was in love with my father. One of the most moving memories I have is when he taught me how to cycle in the garden of my parents' cottage in the Vosges Mountains. All my best memories from early childhood are in those beautiful mountains.

At the end of 1939 he was still fighting on the front lines but he knew the war was lost. He sent us a telegram, saying we must leave immediately. The University was packing up their archives and we were to follow them. At this moment, although our main home was the flat in Strasbourg, we were staying at the cottage in the Vosges.

We had to walk down to the nearest city, Colmar, carrying my paralysed grandmother on a stretcher. From there, someone took us to Strasbourg where the government had organised refugee trains. Each of us was allowed to take twenty kilos, so we each had a suitcase containing only what was really necessary.

This is my first dreadful memory: the refugee trains were bombed by German Messerschmitts. They were very small airplanes. They flew along the trains and dropped bombs. Our train had to stop a few times. Some people would get out, and they were killed on the platform. I saw it all, and it made a deep impression on me. Even now I remember how I started to vomit until my clothes were soaked. My mother took off her pink pullover and put it on me. It was like a dress on me.

That was how we ended up in Clermont Ferrand, a city in the centre of France in a province called Auvergne. God helped us. The big One obviously didn't want us to die: my mother, my grandmother, my sister, my brother and myself, none of us died. But I remained seriously traumatised.

Strasbourg University settled in Clermont Ferrand, in the hopes that the Germans wouldn't reach as far as that. We were sent into a refugee camp for a few days.

The people of Clermont Ferrand were nice to us. Some of them had empty flats which they lent us refugees. An old marquis gave our family an old flat which was rather primitive. He told us, 'You have central heating.' The central heating was in fact a big stove in the middle of the flat! The marquis had false teeth. My brother and I laughed because when he talked you could hear 'bling bling bling'. This is something that, nowadays, sometimes happens to me! All the things we laugh at when we are younger seem to happen to us later.

The marquis had a statue of Joan of Arc in the flat. He had a *plumeau,* a special feather duster he used on her. He said to us, 'See, Joan of Arc's little finger has been broken but I stuck it back on. You must carefully take the dust off her only with this little duster.' He was actually a very nice man.

We stayed there for a while until we found a better flat, and then the city gave us an apartment in a building that wasn't yet finished. The apartment was quite modern. Although nothing was completed it was nice and we were happy there. We were helped by many people who became friends and lent us beds and chairs, and my mother made some pieces of furniture with wooden pallets from vegetable shops.

My father came back from the front and life started again. Then the Armistice was signed and we were absolutely devastated. My father cried when we heard on the radio that General Charles Huntziger had signed the French surrender.

We tried to live as well as we could. My father resumed his job as a physics professor and researcher. My sister resumed her studies as a pharmacist. My brother and I went back to school.

Before we were allocated the flat in the building under construction, we had lived for a while in a nice apartment with a balcony. I still have the memory of the times I spent with my father on the balcony; we often simply remained silent.

One day he suddenly said, 'What are you looking at so intensely?'

'Oh Daddy, I'm trying to see nothing – it's so difficult, though!'

'Well,' he said, 'if you're already thinking of such things at the age of nine, what will you be investigating later on?'

At the beginning we hoped that we would be safe in Clermont Ferrand. The Germans had said that they would leave the south part of France free. The dividing line was a place called Moulins. My father immediately started helping people escape over the frontier there, which was very dangerous because it was guarded by German soldiers. He succeeded in saving quite a few people from the occupied zone.

In 1942 the Germans broke their promise and invaded the whole of France. They established a big centre for the Gestapo near Clermont Ferrand. Nevertheless, my father went on helping people who were trying to resist the occupation.

One day he didn't come home; he just vanished. We enquired and we waited. My father had disappeared together with two or three men who were active in the resistance. Maybe what led to his betrayal was his practice of hiding people in our flat. Strangers would arrive, spend the night and go again in the morning. One man came to stay with us for quite a long time. They called him the Dancer. He helped me do my homework, especially Latin! At the end of the war we heard that he had been arrested and that he may have given names away. Under torture, I'm sure. How could I blame him if it's true that he was responsible? He was a nice man. I think I probably would also give names away if I were tortured.

Most probably my father was shot, because we never saw him again.

We had no money and we had to survive. My mother had no skills, no qualifications: she had just been a housewife and a mother. She had been brought up in a well-to-do family and only knew how to embroider and care for her appearance.

Her parents had been quite rich. My grandfather was a gentleman farmer. He owned a huge piece of land and was successful. When he retired he sold his land with the idea of buying apartment buildings in Strasbourg. However, my grandmother was the one who wore the trousers and my grandfather obeyed her. She had him put all his money in Russian Tsar Bonds to help the Tsar fight the Bolsheviks. Like many people of her generation, my grandmother was afraid of the Communists and the 'yellow peril'! After the revolution in Russia she lost everything and had to live with us.

I think we had always known that my father might disappear one day. He had explained to me that he might be killed, and that it didn't matter at all. What did matter was that Hitler and the Nazis should be eradicated, which would bring about the end of evil. He was sure, as we all were, that once Hitler and the Nazis were gone, everything would be all right and that it would be the best world to live in. None of us imagined that the evil would continue, and even get worse.

My mother was devastated after my father's disappearance because she loved him deeply. Like a little girl, completely and utterly depressed, she stayed in bed, weeping and sleeping. My sister, who was then 22 years old, immediately took a job as an assistant in a pharmacy. Only on Saturdays could she help us at home.

So I found myself, at the age of ten, managing the family. I had to plan the meals and cook. And I had to look after my dying grandmother. Every evening I would brush her long hair and braid it. And every evening she would say, 'Catherine, pray God that I don't wake up tomorrow morning.' Because she also was devastated that my father had disappeared: while she was 76 years old and still alive, my father, aged 52, was gone.

But my mother soon recovered and learned to do everything again, including sewing clothes for us. She found a job in a shop selling hand-knitted baby clothes. She knitted for them, for which she got some money. Later she created little models for them. I helped her. As soon as I came home from school I knitted, knitted and knitted. (I can tell you, I never knitted anything for my own children!) And my brother delivered phone directories on his bicycle. That is how we survived.

There were lots of food restrictions and rationing. We had very little to eat, so that was difficult too. Sometimes my sister and I would cycle up in the mountains to a farm that still had a little produce: a few eggs or a little bit of oil – anything, really. This was the black market, of course, and it was very dangerous. If the Germans caught you on the road with food from the black market you went to jail. So we tried to outsmart them.

One day, I'll never forget it, my sister and I cycled about 30 kilometres. Each of us had two bags attached to our bicycles containing bottles of oil. We were so happy that we were coming back with four bottles of oil. There was no oil left otherwise. When we arrived in front of our apartment building I parked my bicycle. I don't know what went wrong but the bicycle fell over and the bottles fell out. All I could do was watch the oil running into the gutter. I was in tears! Fortunately we still had my sister's two bottles left.

❁

A famous French writer, Jules Romains, wrote a novel called *Poil de Carotte*, 'The Red Haired One', a story about a little orphaned boy. Somewhere in the book he writes: 'Not everyone can be as lucky to be an orphan as I was.' Sometimes I think that is true for me too.

The only real education I had was the love instilled in me by my father; after that my education was finished. And while I had the example of my mother's tenderness, I received no education about how to behave. Of course we were a bourgeois family: there were manners which I copied. I could see for myself how people functioned. But apart from that – physical questions, sexual questions – nothing was imposed on me. I found everything out on the street and with friends. In some ways it helped that I was not given any limits, except love and respect for others. When I hear my friends talking about their childhoods and all the rules and principles that blocked them later in life, I realise that I had had nothing of the sort.

Religion wasn't a hindrance either. We were Protestant. At our parish in Strasbourg there were two pastors. They used to fight and say nasty things about each other. My father got really angry. One day he said, 'I'm not going to attend a service anymore in a church where the role models are fighting.' He walked out of the church and we never went back.

I had an interesting relationship with one of the pastors, because he was more like a philosopher. I regarded my confirmation at the age of fourteen as simply a philosophical dialogue with this interesting minister.

During our five years in Clermont Ferrand, I met two people who deeply influenced me: a young couple who belonged to the Salvation Army and were truly living Jesus Christ's teachings. They lived with their children in a big attic with no furniture other than many beds. Their home was open to everyone including homeless people, although there were not so many around at that time. A lot of poor people came to them and they fed them and loved them with a pure and disinterested love. I became friends with them and often stayed at their place. If I ever had role models, it was my father and this couple. I've never seen Christians truly living their faith as these people did. My new neighbour here in Montpellier asked me the other day, 'Do you have a religion?' I said, 'If I have one, it's just Jesus Christ's message: that's what I believe in.'

Soon some flats in our building were given to French collaborators and I discovered the absurdity and horror of war again. These collaborators were protected by German SS soldiers who were on guard in the basement. My bicycle was also in the basement. When I went down for it one day, suddenly this huge man appeared around the corner with his gun pointing at me. I came just up to his hips where I could see his belt. *Gott mit uns* was inscribed on the belt. 'God with us!' I was shocked when I saw this. Eventually they got to know me and I got used to them, but it was a difficult situation, these French people collaborating with the Germans. In the flat below them, twice a day we listened to the BBC for the news from General de Gaulle, with the radio hidden under an eiderdown to muffle the sound, for it was strictly forbidden to do so and punished with imprisonment.

I didn't realise at the time how many collaborators there were. I only discovered this recently in a French documentary on television.

As I said before, in a way my upbringing imposed on me no limits. As children often do, I already felt that we are all one. I felt that with everyone. Sometimes people were shocked because I, a little girl of ten years old, would say to a gentleman of 60, 'Hallo, how are you?' just as if we were peers of the same age. I didn't see the difference between them and me, you see! I felt basically we were all the same!

The idea of wanting to become an actress started in Clermont Ferrand. I thought I could be anything! I had two school friends and together we wrote little plays. We also performed them and had so much fun.

The war ended when I was fifteen. During our so-called liberation I had a second shock about the absurdity of war.

There had been two movements of French resistance. One was the Communists who had been fighting against the Nazis in Germany and also resisted them in France; they were the first people who were sent to the concentration camps. The other movement was called *Francs-Tireurs et Partisans*. What happened after the Liberation was what they call in France *le Règlement de Comptes* (the settling of accounts). People who didn't like each other for whatever reason accused one another of being pro-Nazi. These people were then ill-treated by the so-called liberators, when often they had done nothing!

The Gestapo had been very clever when they left. On a desk in their headquarters they had left a list with names.

These stupid men from the French resistance saw this list and assumed these people were collaborators. They killed practically all of them, although those people had not been collaborators at all – they had been part of the resistance! Of course the Germans had thought that this would happen.

The French Partisans also ill-treated women who were accused of having been friendly to German soldiers or having made love to them. They shaved these women in the streets and swung their bodies over fires. When I saw that I went home and cried. I was disgusted, it was horrible. I learned something about the human species then. To think that one side is dark and evil and the other side is good is a great mistake!

I remember how we, my best school friends and I, were so happy when we put on our blue, white and red clothes, the colours of the French flag, in celebration. But when we saw these scenes going on in the streets we returned home in tears. My mother was as sorry as I was. She said, 'Well, that's life. Humankind is like that.' It was a terrible disillusionment.

One night I had been weeping for a long time when suddenly the weeping stopped. I found myself in light, in wonderful loving light. All reasons to cry had vanished.

I discovered that this Light is life, real life, and we need to be silent to see it. Human beings are too busy, too noisy to hear the silence, to see the Light.

For months it remained alive in me and then it slowly vanished. But from then on I knew it existed. I knew that it was there, and that it was real.

2

The Light within

The next morning when I enter the elevator to go up to Catherine's apartment I meet three other senior residents. 'Aaahhh, une amie de Catherine!' they conclude right away, smiling. Apparently all foreign and unusual visitors in this building are 'amies de Catherine', friends of Catherine.

The door of her apartment is open. 'Allo!' I call when I let myself in. 'Allo!' I hear from the bathroom. When she comes out she is still in pyjamas. Her nurse has not yet arrived. For more than a month she has not been able to lift her right arm and needs help to get dressed and undressed.

When the nurse arrives they disappear into the bedroom. When they reappear Catherine is wearing a t-shirt and trousers as colourful as her apartment. She looks in the mirror. 'Oh my God, I am naked!' she laughs and grabs her earrings to put them on.

We chat and joke over breakfast. Then we clear the kitchen table.

'So, when the war ended ...' I say ...

… we went back to Strasbourg. We arrived into a difficult situation because the city had been occupied by the Germans. France and Germany had been fighting over the territory of Alsace-Lorraine for centuries: at one time the poor people were Germans and another time French. As soon as the Germans had won control in 1939, they had declared Alsace-Lorraine to be German. They closed the frontiers and everyone was supposed to speak German; it was forbidden to speak French. My uncle and aunt couldn't leave Strasbourg as we had done because they ran a posh pâtisserie. Later my aunt went to prison because she was speaking French, can you imagine?

So I was ill at ease, because everybody was still speaking German or Alsatian, a regional dialect. I felt like a stranger. All of us who came back from inner France (they called us 'inner French') felt lost. We had nothing left because the Germans had seized everything. The flat my parents had rented before we left was empty. I think they had put German families in the apartments, and when they moved back to Germany they had taken everything with them. We didn't know what to do. Luckily we got help.

A middle-aged woman who had been the University librarian was a friend of ours, and when the Germans arrived in 1942 and arrested all the Alsatian students and teachers, this librarian was also taken away. (My sister was lucky that she wasn't there during the arrests.) Everyone was sent to the concentration camps. I think the Germans wanted to re-establish Strasbourg as the famous German University it once had been.

My father, however, had succeeded in getting this woman out of the camp. She was rich and owned several houses in Strasbourg. One of them was an old historic building which had been turned into apartments, and she gave us one of these to live in.

We had very little money; my mother got only half of the pension my father would have had when he retired, so we all started doing jobs to help her.

My body had suffered as a result of the war. I was weak and completely deficient in calcium due to the poor quality of the food I'd been eating in my growing years. In fact, we had eaten practically nothing except potatoes. The Red Cross went around the schools and selected children who were in a particularly bad condition. I was one of them, and I was sent to Geneva. Two Swiss families looked after me: I spent a month with each that summer.

The first family was especially wonderful: in fact, they overfed me. They were the Platis and they were Italian Swiss. They were working-class people and lived on the seventh floor of a high building. At first I could scarcely eat at all, my stomach had shrunk so much. So, after the first course, the father took me down the stairs, all seven floors of them, and then all seven floors up again. Then they served me the second course.

Their system worked well. I ate so much that I had grown about ten centimetres at the end of those two months. And I had put on weight and my breasts had developed.

When I came back in the train to France, my mother was waiting for me on the platform. She didn't recognise me; she passed by me without seeing me, so greatly had I been transformed by these families' treatment. I really owe them my life. Even so, my body never completely recovered from the war; it has remained weak my whole life.

I returned to Switzerland twice as a young girl. A friend of my mother's gave her the name of a Swiss couple who were looking for an au pair. For two summers I went to work in

Biel, which I enjoyed. They were an old couple, very kind, and we got along well. And Switzerland is so beautiful. To thank me for my help, they took me on coach trips high up among the mountains and glaciers.

While I was studying for my baccalauréat in Strasbourg, a wonderful event in the history of world citizenship occurred. It was 1947, and the presidents of countries from all over the world came to Les Invalides, an ancient monument close to the Eiffel Tower. The area was declared international no-man's land, and there they began to establish the United Nations.

A young American also arrived in Paris at this time. He tore up his identity papers and said, 'This is ridiculous. You are inventing countries. Countries are not a natural thing. They result in awful wars. You say this is no-man's land, so I am entitled to stay here. This is where I belong.' And he pitched his tent right there.

His name was Garry Davis and he had flown one of the planes that had dropped the bombs on Hiroshima. Most of these pilots never recovered from their guilt but Garry Davis was awakened by his experience. He was an activist for a world government and world citizenship. I think the movement still continues; some people have world citizen passports. At that time many people were involved, serious people like economists who were thinking in terms of a world economy.

Garry had great charisma. All of us students were thrilled by him. I went to Paris to see him and we students congregated around Garry the whole time. He caused such a stir that the police got worried. The chief of police and the prime minister came to debate with him, but Garry had trained himself in Gandhi's dialectic: he was very kind, stayed calm and brought the person who was speaking to him to contradict himself.

He drove the authorities crazy because they couldn't persuade him – he persuaded them! He used their own words to show that they were wrong. Our excitement grew!

News of the turmoil surrounding Garry was always on the radio, and young German students heard about it on the other side of the Rhine. They put up their tents by the Rhine and asked Garry to come to them.

Eventually Garry was told by the Ministry of Internal Affairs that he wasn't allowed to stay in Paris anymore, so he walked to Strasbourg. So I went back to Strasbourg too, to my mother's. Garry pitched his tent beside the Rhine. He had an old tent about a metre wide. He said, 'You say there is one country here and one country there. Obviously there is at least a line dividing them, so I am allowed to camp on it.' And the whole story started up again. Both students and many other people came and gathered around Garry. The police were *sur les dents* as we say in France, or 'on their teeth', meaning they got really nervous.

I'd loved the English language from the time I started learning it at school when I was ten or eleven years old. It's strange but I felt as if I was recovering something familiar, as if this language were a part of me. So at the end of my *lycée* I could speak English, not very well but well enough. Therefore I was able to help Garry by being his translator with the police and other people. We became really close. One day he came to my mother's flat. The police parked in front of my mother's house because, as they say here in France, 'When a man is causing problems, look for the woman behind him.' Of course my mother was very upset.

Unfortunately, winter came, and Garry, still in his tent, caught pneumonia and was taken to hospital. No one could explain what exactly happened but when he came out he was not the same. To me he was like a lamp that had gone out. I couldn't understand it; maybe they had done something to his brain. He was sent back to America, and later, I read a ridiculous story in a newspaper that he had been arrested for stealing a bra in a supermarket.

So Garry never got to Germany. We were all sorry. I was particularly sad because, of course, I was in love with him, although I knew he had a fiancée in New York. I did not want to get intimately involved with him, but when he disappeared, I was devastated.

After all this had happened, what with the war and the loss of my father and other people who had been shot, I fell into a deep depression. I was sixteen. I remember walking along the river and wanting to put an end to my life. 'There's no point in living,' I thought. Then I thought of my mother ... What saved me then and has always helped me in my life is crying. I spent hours weeping in my room at night so that my mother wouldn't see.

One night I was in tears again but suddenly the weeping stopped. I found myself in light, in wonderful loving light. All reasons to cry had vanished.

I discovered that this is life, real life. We need to be silent to see it. Human beings are too busy, too noisy; they can't hear the silence, they can't see the Light.

For months afterwards I walked on little clouds. The experience remained very alive within me. Then slowly, slowly, it vanished. I lost it because I didn't have the means to see it at will. Later Douglas' experiments would give me the means, *des moyens utiles*; 'useful means' as the Buddhists say, a way to get to see the Light.

I tried to share my vision with other people: 'There is another reality here which is luminous Light and silence. There is too much noise, and so you can't hear and see what is real.' But of course everybody laughed at me and said, 'She's a strange girl. It's adolescence. Wait till she grows up, it will pass.'

But from then on I knew it existed. Even though I couldn't find it anymore, I knew it was there. That helped me immensely throughout my life because whenever I was in a bad situation, which was often the case, I knew it was there and that it was real.

I loved the language so much that I wanted to improve my English. My mother found me a summer job in England through a friend. A rich family, called Holmes, was looking for a French au pair to look after their children. They lived in Lynton in Devon, so I went there for two months.

When I arrived I realised that what they wanted me to do was not so much look after the two children (who were actually teenagers), but be their maid. The family had a large estate. The father had been wounded during the first world war as a result of which he was a little crazy. He couldn't work anymore. His wife was wonderful. She was a musician, she played the organ. To get an income they had turned their property into a guesthouse. They needed someone to serve early tea, to clean the rooms and to serve evening meals.

At first I thought, 'Oh my goodness, I'm not going to stay!' Then I thought of my mother who had saved the money for the long and expensive train journey. So I decided: 'I'm not going to let her down. I will stay and learn English.' And stay I did!

Not long afterwards the charming lady of the family fell ill. She was taken to hospital and I was left on my own. Before she left home, she said, 'Please, Catherine, will you stay? The whole house is in your hands. My husband is too crazy to take the guests' money. You have to do it – it's all we'll have for the whole winter!' Every Saturday new guests would arrive and the old guests would leave and pay their money, you see. So I found myself doing everything, including ordering food and dealing with the people who made the deliveries. At that time there were still rationing cards in England so, as you can imagine, I had no choice but to learn English.

One aspect of the husband's craziness was that he collected *pendules* (or clocks), which he kept in the attic. Not just alarm clocks, but big antique clocks centuries old. As soon as he had some money he went to antique shops and bought a clock or two or three. He was obsessed about getting all these old clocks to ring at the same time.

Whenever I found myself alone with him for a moment, he would say: 'You bastard French woman! You're taking all the money!' He hated me and wanted me to give the money back.

Many funny things happened to me there. The father was so crazy (and even his wife was a little so) that they accepted more people than they had rooms for. A few days before the Saturday when new guests would arrive, he would build a hut in the park. Soon I had to give up my room and live in one of those huts. There were giant spiders in them, coming in from the woods, so I was very scared. Even the children had to give up their rooms.

I had to do everything: I had to get up early in the morning, bring early tea to all the guests and clean the rooms. A little later on they also had me cook the meals. 'Oh you are French, you can cook!'

The family had a big white long-haired pedigree dog from the Pyrenees. When he stood on his back legs he was taller than me. The mother loved that dog so much that she did everything he wanted; he was pretty spoiled. His name was Zaza.

One day I had made soup and I was preparing to serve it in

the dining room. In those days people still went to supper in evening dress. Between the kitchen and the dining room was a door, and the dog was lying in the doorway. I stood there with the big soup tureen on my tray. I said, 'Zaza, please get up!' He wouldn't move. Finally, I tried to step over him and tripped as he got to his feet! The soup splashed all over people's fine clothing. Fortunately, the guests didn't blame me. I think they realised I did everything in the house and were moved by my situation. But I did learn fluent English, in two months!

At the end of my stay one of the guest families invited me to spend two weeks with them in London. The mother was a French lady, a cello player, and she was very sorry for me. 'Oh Catherine,' she said, 'that you have to go through all this!' 'No, no,' I said, 'it's all right!'

To make up for it they invited me to their home in Bayswater. They offered me everything possible in those two weeks. I was lucky, it was so nice to discover London! So that was my English summer adventure!

I passed my baccalauréat in 1949 and won a competition for a scholarship in the United States called the Fulbright Scholarship. Mr Fulbright, a wealthy man, had left his fortune to help students who had been victims of the war. I was sent to a university in North Carolina. I went by ship, the *Queen Elizabeth*, on the way out, and later I returned on the *France*. It was a fascinating experience.

America was an absolute paradise. In France we still had food rationing; in the States everything was plentiful. You had a coin, put it in a machine and out came a bottle of Coke or a sandwich, just like that. And oranges! I had never yet seen an orange. Orange juice – fantastic! I had a wonderful time. Everybody was nice to me, I felt blessed.

On the ship my trunk got lost so when I arrived at the university I had no clothes, nothing. I was accommodated in a freshman dorm and all the girls came to say hello. When they heard the news about my trunk they said, 'Come to our rooms and help yourself. Take any dress you want.' It was almost a pity that my trunk arrived two or three days later.

I was very successful at the university. There are freshmen, sophomores, juniors and seniors at American universities, and I soon realised that, although I was a freshman, my level was really that of the juniors. Because French education was much tougher in those days, you learned things younger than they did in the States. What they were doing at freshman level we did in France when we were twelve years old.

I studied American English, American history and literature. I also took economics because I wanted to understand economic issues. And I discovered they had courses in drama! In America you can graduate in drama and become an actress that way. I subscribed for the course, hoping to learn more about acting. A theatre company with two lady directors invited me to come and act for them. I hesitated.

'I can speak English, but with my accent?'

'We'll train and help you,' they said.

A teacher from the university who spoke French fluently said he would train me to improve my pronunciation. I was fascinated by the theatre and enjoyed acting a lot. We performed a few modern plays. One of them was *The House of Bernarda Alba* by Garcia Lorca.

Although my scholarship paid for everything, my mother had not been able to give me any extra so I had no pocket money. In those days every small town in America had its own newspaper with its own journalists. When anything happened they were immediately informed about it, so they knew that a French girl had arrived in town. Soon I found a job through the local newspaper.

All the journalists came to interview me. You can imagine, I felt like a celebrity. I got many phone calls: 'Oh, a French girl! Would you like to come out? I'm inviting you over tonight.' All the guys in town wanted to meet a French girl. Some of them told me that they were absolutely certain that all French girls were very easy to get into bed. They also thought that French people drank wine all day long, from breakfast onwards!

I told one of the journalists that I was looking for a job. Soon I was offered a post at Montaldo's, a big department store like Marks and Spencer but of superior quality. It was the beginning of what they called *prêt-à-porter* or ready-to-wear dresses, when the top dressmakers in Paris began to make available at a cheaper price limited copies of unique, haut-couture items. I was hired to model them, and I was paid very well for it.

In the summer a few American student friends and I were offered jobs on an island off the east coast of North Carolina. The island was owned by a billionaire, Mr Ray T Adams, who was known as 'the king of canned meat'. Incredibly, they managed to stuff a whole cooked chicken or turkey into a can. They also made this horrible army food, like corned beef.

Mr Adams had an old Irish-style house on the island – I couldn't call it a cottage because it was big – which he used as a private hotel with important guests from the American government. It was obviously for business reasons, because he received big orders for his canned meat from them. He took them wild duck hunting on the island, and in the summer he used students as hostesses for his government guests.

Although he was 52 years old he liked me and wanted to marry me. Of course I said, 'I can't marry you. I am not in love with you. Can't you see how different we are?' He was such a nice man that he didn't change his attitude towards me when I said no.

When I left after the summer, I told him I had a brother

with a big problem: he was extremely shy. So shy, in fact, that he failed his exams because he lost the means to express himself. My mother was very worried. Mr Adams paid for my brother's passage to the States and gave him a job. Thanks to him my brother learned to speak fluent English. When he came back to France, he immediately found a job because not many people could speak English at that time.

Mr Adams would have given him a job so that he could have stayed in the States. At first I couldn't understand why he didn't accept. My brother was a reserved man, and you never knew what he was really feeling. But then I guessed. On his desk stood a picture of a woman – and one day it was gone. I think he had a *chagrin d'amour*, a love sorrow, in the States. So he came back to Strasbourg and lived there ever after.

At the end of my scholarship I returned to Strasbourg to my mother. She was a real darling and loved me very much but living with her was quite suffocating. I wanted to be away for a while. Not knowing where exactly I was going, I left for a holiday on the west coast of France. I had little money so I went by bus. On the way I visited some friends in Nantes and went to the tourist office. There I saw a photograph of a place which struck me like a blow to the chest.

'That is where I want to go!' I thought.

'Where is this? How do you get there?' I asked.

They told me that it was a small island called Île d'Yeu, the Island of God. 'There is a boat twice a week from a small port. If you miss it you have to wait for the next one,' they said.

I took a bus to the small port. I had to wait a few days for the next boat and I found an abandoned factory where I slept in my sleeping bag. It was such an adventure. When the boat left the French coast, the captain was drunk. He didn't manoeuvre the boat well and we got stuck on a sandbank just outside the port. The tide was going out so we couldn't move. We spent the whole night on the boat, which was such fun. We played cards in the moonlight and got to know each other. I immediately became friendly with a painter. He said, 'I'm going to show you Île d'Yeu. It is marvellous, you'll see!'

When the tide came in, we sailed to the island. We arrived at five in the morning. The only café in the port was already open; they had been waiting for us with hot coffee and croissants. They called us the shipwrecked ones, saved from drowning.

As soon as we had eaten, the painter, whose name I have forgotten, said, 'Now we're going to walk to the place you have seen on your photograph.' The island is very small, about five kilometres wide and twenty kilometres long. We walked right across the island in the light of a marvellous rising sun.

On the other side we came to a small fishing port. The painter took me to a café owned by a huge lady. She looked like a gypsy woman, or maybe she was Spanish. It was so funny because she had this little husband, very short and thin, and she was certainly the one who wore the trousers. She shouted at me, 'What are you doing here? A young girl like you, all alone and wearing trousers!' Yes, I was wearing trousers because I'd come back from America with the first jeans. Everybody joined in: 'Ah! A girl of your age wearing trousers! What a crazy girl!'

In fact, she became my best friend. She immediately found me a place to sleep, a room close to her house, owned by an old lady. The old lady said to me, 'Oh, you come from the continent! Tell me, my little girl, has the war ended?' This was in 1950, so you can imagine just how far away this island was from civilization. Later, when I went there with my Moroccan husband, they said, 'Oh! Are you from Morocco?

Do they have the moon in Morocco?' It's all changed now, of course; now they know more.

These people were still so nice at that time; money didn't exist for them. Some fed me fish, and one of them lent me a bike. I cycled all over the island: every path, every beach, everywhere. It was enchanting. I completely fell in love with the island; it was pure beauty. One side has high cliffs with enormous waves dashing up against them, sending up a flurry of foam. The other side is flat with sandy beaches and pine trees, flanked by rocks at each end. The people lived by fishing for tuna and lobsters. That too is now finished: it's been ruined by those huge industrial ships that collect up all the fish and deep-freeze it. Anyway, that's another story. Île d'Yeu became my second home.

After I left the island I moved to Paris to finish my English studies. My mother was terrified that I would become an actress because in those days they earned almost no money in theatres. To reassure her I went on with my English degrees and, fortunately, I got all the necessary certificates. I owe her a lot for that, because later in life that helped me to earn my living as an English teacher.

I got to the level where I should have been writing a thesis but I didn't want to continue: I still wanted to be an actress. I was attending a few courses with a famous actor called Fernand Ledoux who gave free courses at the Sorbonne; the drama schools were extremely expensive, too expensive for me. I also played a few roles in a theatre in Paris.

Then I met my husband, the father of my children.

In winter it gets very cold on Île d'Yeu. Driss and I were so poor that we had to share the only big warm woollen winter coat we had. So we couldn't go out together: we always took it in turns.

Then somebody gave us one of those grey woollen blankets used by the French army. Driss, who was so talented in many ways, cut a coat from it for me. He managed to find someone with a sewing machine who sewed it together. When it was ready everybody was amazed because it looked like a coat 'grande couture'. It really was beautiful.

So by the end of the winter I had my own coat!

3
The night watchman

Catherine's apartment is located on the top floor of the retirement block. Her balcony faces south, big and sunny and overlooking Montpellier. In the distance, between the tall buildings on the horizon, I see a small strip of the Mediterranean. 'That is where I first lived when I returned to France after Douglas died,' she says, pointing at Palavas-les-Flots.

Her balcony is covered with flowering plants. She loves flowers; she says they are her remedy for the pain of her arthritis. Her daughter brought up a big orange tree yesterday which now lives in a huge pot in the corner. Its blooms smell like sweet perfume.

The phone rings. I come to discover that it often does. For a long time I hear the sound of rapid melodious French. It must be one of her children or grandchildren. I make myself tea and sit down between the flowers, enjoying life as it is happening here, right before my eyes: all the way from the closest bloom to the small strip of blue, far off where the sea meets the sky.

Nothing to do but wait till she is ready to continue.

How I met Driss was just as I met Douglas – just like that! I was living in a cheap attic room. Some friends from America sent me a telegram saying that they were coming to Paris. 'We want to see you so please book a hotel room for us near you.' So that's what I did.

There was a hotel on the opposite side of the street. A friend of mine who was visiting and I went downstairs and crossed the boulevard. It was seven o'clock in the evening and the night watchman, a young man, was already there.

My friend said to me, 'We must hurry, you know you have an appointment with Jean-Louis Barrault.'

Jean-Louis Barrault was a well-known actor and director.

'I could call him if I had his phone number,' I said.

The night watchman took out his address book, opened it and said, 'Do you want Jean-Louis Barrault's phone number? Here it is.'

I looked in his address book and saw the names of many people I knew from show business.

I asked, 'How do you know all these people?'

'I am from Morocco,' he said, 'and I have become a writer. I've just finished my first book and my publisher introduced me to these people.'

It was love at first sight.

He immediately said, 'Would you have a cup of coffee with me tomorrow?'

I was impressed: he was very handsome, charming and obviously brilliant. So I said yes. From then on we were never apart.

The next day we had coffee together and it was magical. Driss had no money and was very thin, like a skeleton really. His father had sent him to Paris to study. He wanted him to become a doctor, but Driss was obsessed with becoming a writer. So his father had stopped sending him money and wanted him to come back to Morocco. That was why Driss was doing this job, security in a hotel. He would work at night and write his book in the daytime.

It was June when I met Driss. My mother was up in the cottage in the Vosges Mountains which I've already mentioned. An Irish woman had built it and when she left France she sold it to my father. It was a marvellous place, right on top of a mountain. Far below was the Rhine valley, and in the distance you could see Germany and the whole of the Rhine plain. It was stunning.

During the war the cottage had been practically destroyed: the area had been a battleground. The Allied forces would overcome the Germans and then the Germans would fight back; so they continued, back and forth and back and forth. Our cottage was right in the middle of all this and it had been used as a headquarters. When the war was over the place was ruined. The roof was gone, the walls had big holes from the gunfire and everywhere inside was blood. When we came back to Strasbourg after the war my mother had no money to fix it but some friends helped us to clean up.

During my studies in Paris I had met an American historian from Harvard who had written his thesis about General de Gaulle. He had had the thesis approved in America but he also wanted French approval. He advertised for a translator at the university where I was studying. I saw his request and applied for the work. He tested my proficiency and then offered me the job. It was my first translation: a book about General De Gaulle! It made me a lot of money, which I gave to my mother to rebuild the cottage roof.

I called my mother in the Vosges and told her I had met a guy. I explained who Driss was and how weak his health was.

'Let him come here immediately,' she said.

'We don't have any money,' I replied.

'I'll send the money for train tickets.'

So we went to my mother's up in the mountains and she fell in love with Driss too. My whole family fell in love with him – at first! He was so pleasant and likeable and persuasive. He had this gift that many Africans have: he was a good storyteller. At the moment he was a novelist but originally he would have been a wonderful storyteller. He could tell you the most moving story about anything, even a fridge or whatever, and you would be charmed by every word he said. My mother really adored him.

Pretty soon, though, she realised that he wasn't exactly the son-in-law she was dreaming of. He didn't have the same rhythm. He wouldn't do the things he was asked to do. If you asked him to please take the rubbish bin out, he would do it once, twice – and then never again. Or he would lie in bed in the mornings, or do other things artists do.

But it took a long time for my mother to lose confidence in him entirely and not to love him anymore.

I didn't intend to marry him. I thought that because I was going to be an actress and he was going to be a writer there would be no need to marry. But my brother and my mother, still in love with him at that point, wanted us to marry. One day everybody arrived with presents for our so-called engagement celebration. I was too young to know any better and I accepted the situation, mostly to satisfy my mother. I didn't see the problem I was getting into, and I was very much in love, so eventually we got married in Strasbourg.

I was twenty-one and he was around that age too. We never

knew his age exactly because in his country they had no civil records. When the French colonialists wanted to catalogue the population they went around asking everyone for their birth date. People would say something like 'He was born when the bougainvillea was in flower' or 'He was born when such and so happened'. That's how they fixed an approximate birth date for Driss.

I wanted to continue with my acting and Driss wanted to be with me, so we went back to Paris. Of course we never had any money. I was living on a meagre scholarship and Driss had very little too. In one way it was hard living together in Paris, but it wasn't too difficult for us because we were in love.

Sometimes we had nothing to eat so we both got very thin. One day some friends gave us a packet of rice. We had a little kerosene stove and a pan, so I cooked the rice and we were looking forward to having a meal. But when I tried to drain off the water the lid of the pan slid off. Silently we watched all the rice going down the drain. Our friends said that we'd become so thin that we could pass between a poster and a wall without unsticking the poster! Lots of funny and enjoyable things happened to us in Paris, but we were always hungry!

I knew Driss was going to be a great writer and his first book was successful; he was immediately recognised by the critics. Unfortunately, however, his subject matter did not interest the French people at all. This was 1952, and he had written a critique of both the laws of Islam and the way he was brought up, and French colonialism. The result was that he was spurned by both sides. Morocco had not gained its independence at that time and the Muslim Brotherhood had a lot of power. When they read his book they declared a *fatwa* against him.

They did not yet have the means to pursue him in France, but they said that if he set foot on Moroccan ground, they would immediately kill him. So we couldn't go to Morocco.

Meanwhile we lived in a room on the top floor of a cheap hotel. Very often we had not paid the rent so we would hide in our room; we wouldn't go out in case the receptionist saw us.

Driss earned some money from his book. As soon as he received it he came back with a wonderful ring for me. It had a zircon, which looks like a diamond but is of lesser value. He had spent all his money.

'Are you mad? We need to pay the rent!' I said.

'Ah yes ... I had forgotten!'

That was the kind of guy he was. So I went back to the shop and said that my husband was crazy and would they please take the ring back because we couldn't afford it. Fortunately they did. This was the kind of thing he did; he never came down to reality.

At first we were involved with show business society in Paris but pretty soon we got fed up with these people. There was lots of hypocrisy amongst the writers and actors. They all used to pat each other on the back as if they were best friends.

Of course, with Driss being a Muslim, even though he never practised, and a North African, he was looked down on by French writers. Also they were jealous of his literary success – and his success with women, because all the women fell in love with him.

We left Paris in somewhat strange circumstances. I saw a little advertisement in *Le Monde,* the famous French newspaper. Someone in a village in the south of France was looking for a couple to live with him and help him look after his goats.

We decided that that was exactly what we needed. In two hours we had packed and off we went to the village to look after goats!

As soon as we arrived I thought, 'Oh my goodness!' The farm was half in ruins and the man was filthy. He was an old retired major. I don't know why he was all alone on his farm. He stank, almost as badly as the male goats. I don't know if you have ever encountered the smell of goats: it's lethal! Our room was at the top of a part of the farm that was still standing. The toilets were in the attic. They were actually holes in the wooden floor. You had to sit there and everything fell down into a stable, so they also stank.

Soon we decided we couldn't possibly stay there. We wept in each other's arms. On top of it all, I was vomiting all the time, and soon I realised I was pregnant. It was strange because we had been together for four years without using contraception. There was nothing available in France – no pills, nothing – and I had never become pregnant before now. In fact, I'd thought that I was sterile, that I would never be pregnant. Maybe the cause was psychological because at the time I had wanted so badly to be an actress, an ambition which had now faded. Now I was in love and the possibility of having a child had returned. After this I got pregnant almost every year.

We told the major that we were going to leave. The village was practically empty; all the people had had to leave because of poverty. We found a small empty apartment in a half-ruined house. It was the winter of 1957. It was terrible, I've never been so cold in my whole life. The mistral, a strong wind that blows in the South of France, can suddenly cause winter temperatures to drop right down, and the villagers had no proper way of heating their houses. We only had a fireplace and we didn't have any money to buy wood, so we went into the fields and collected wood from the vines. Even so, the fire only warmed our legs and bellies.

That village is posh now. All the ruins were bought by Parisian artists and it became a wonderful tourist destination full of artists and art shops. Driss and I watched them as they began to arrive. He wrote a short story about them, *De Tous Les Horizons*. It's in a collection of short stories which I think is his best, his masterpiece.

❁

I got into a state of despair and called my mother.

'I don't know what to do. Can we go to your cottage in the mountains?' I asked her.

She said yes of course. We went immediately north to the Vosges. The weather was cold there too, but that house was prepared for cold weather. We had big earthenware wood stoves and lots of wood, and we were warm! We had a beautiful time up there. The snow was up to our waists and the sky was blue over forests of blue-green fir trees. There was a mist in the valley and over the River Rhine below. It was an enchanting world.

When it was time for Laurence to be born we went down to Strasbourg. I gave birth to her at a nice maternity unit. We were all extremely happy: she was so beautiful. It was the time when the first satellite had been launched around the Earth. It was called 'Sputnik', a Russian word meaning 'companion', so we called baby Laurence Sputnik! Her father was crazy about her. She became a pretty and cheerful child.

It was also around this time that my mother began to dislike my husband. He would spend most of his time writing; he wouldn't join in with family life. In fact, my whole bourgeois family – my sister, my brother-in-law, the uncles, aunts and everyone – started turning against him. I couldn't bear it because I was still in love with him.

We couldn't move immediately so when Laurence was still

a baby I applied for a job as a teacher at a place near Strasbourg. It was awful when I began the job: I'd had no training at all and I didn't know how to teach. All of a sudden I found myself in front of a class of young men just a few years younger than me. But I slowly learnt and carried on with it for a while, and Driss went on writing. He refused to take up any other form of livelihood except writing. He made no money and he was no help in the house. He wanted to write – full-stop. No wonder my family didn't appreciate him. But I believed in love beyond barriers.

'I must show you the country of my heart,' I had said when I'd met Driss, so I had introduced him already to Île d'Yeu. We decided to go back to the island with Laurence, who was ten months old, after I had finished teaching that year. At that time you could still live on the island with very little money. We rented an old house for a few francs a month and we went on working. Driss wrote his second book. He took it to his publisher in Paris and got some money for it. I translated American articles for a famous American magazine based in Paris called *Preuves*. So we had a little income to survive on the island, which was wonderful. To us, life was a marvel.

Our house was very basic. We had to go to a well for water, and we had to go to the side of the house for the toilet. And we had no electricity, just oil lamps. But we were full of wonder and our baby was fine, so it was no problem. The only problem was that I fell pregnant again, and I didn't feel like having a baby on the island: the only doctor was drunk half of the time.

So, a year after we'd arrived, I decided to go back to Strasbourg to have my second baby there. Of course we went to my mother's. She always took us in. But we didn't stay in Strasbourg: we went up to the cottage in the Vosges Mountains with Laurence. It was winter again, and high up in the mountains, the snow was up to our waists again. The farmers in the Vosges cut lanes out of the snowbanks so that you could get from place to place.

One day I said to Driss, 'I think the baby's coming. I'll have to go down.' He was going to stay to look after Laurence.

I walked all the way down from the mountains and then I hitchhiked. A lorry stopped for me and took me to a small town called Colmar. I had already told the hospital there that I was going to have a baby, and they had promised to take me in. The lorry driver was very nice. He took me straight to the clinic. And the next day, on December 28th, Stephan was born.

He was a wonderful baby boy with bright eyes. He looked like his father, and so I called him '*petit* Driss'. A week later I went back up to the mountains with my new baby, and again we had a happy time up there. We were surrounded by stunning natural scenery, we were still in love, we had two lovely babies and we were doing well.

In spite of the excellent Alsatian wood stoves in every room, I was always complaining that I was cold. Driss got tired of this. One day he told this story:

'Catherine was always cold so Driss said, "We will move to the South of France." "Oh yes, very good!" Catherine replied. But in the South of France she was still cold. So he said, "We can buy you a fur coat!" They bought her a fur coat but still she was cold. Then he said, "Let's live in Africa!" They went to Africa. Still cold. "We'll go to the equator!" Nothing helped. And Catherine got so desperate that she committed suicide.

'When she arrived in heaven St Peter welcomed her. However, when he heard that she had committed suicide he could not let her enter paradise. It was against the rules. But since he knew that she had always been a good woman and had never hurt anyone or anything, he thought, "I can't put this woman in hell. I'll put her in paradise anyway."

'So he did. He told her, "I am not supposed to put you in paradise but I'll do it anyway. You actually should be in the other place." "What's the other place?" Catherine asked. "Well, it's a bad place," St Peter answered. "There is eternal fire there and it's really hot. There is a lot of suffering – and you don't deserve that."

'A few days later he was still thinking about that lady and went to see how she was doing. When she saw him she said, "Oh please, I am so cold here. Could you not put me in the other place where you said there is fire and high heat?" "But you might suffer!" "No no, please, take me there!" So he took her to hell. When he closed the door of hell, St Peter was very unhappy. He thought, "This poor woman doesn't deserve to be here."

'The next day, as soon as he could, he went to hell to see what was happening. When he opened hell's door he immediately heard this loud shout: "Shut that door!"

'And of course he knew who was shouting!'

A year later I got pregnant again. Our financial situation was getting worse and worse. It was all getting too much. We went down to Strasbourg to have the baby. I went to the hospital at the right time but there were too many women there waiting to deliver. The midwife in charge thought my labour was taking too long, so she gave me an injection to hurry things up.

The result of this was that the poor baby was literally thrown out. Because his brain, having been compressed, expanded too quickly, it haemorrhaged.

I was very emotional when they came and said, 'Do you want to have another look at him again before we take him away?'

I asked what had happened and they showed me the baby in a glass box. Of course it was an incubator, but to me it looked like a glass coffin. I was in a panic. Poor Daniel, what bad luck! But he has acquired some wisdom along the way and tells me now, 'It was my fate.'

They took him to the children's hospital in Strasbourg. I was devastated, and very worried about what was going to happen to him. They kept him there for weeks. I couldn't touch him, I could only see him through a panel of glass. He was given antibiotics and well looked after, but I'm sure he suffered greatly from not having immediate physical contact with his mother. When he came out of hospital, we looked after him as well as possible but he turned out to be a difficult baby: he always wanted something different. You could see how, young as he was, he resisted everything – which was quite understandable. I understand it now, but in those days I didn't. I was very unhappy, being unable to satisfy him.

The situation with my family in Strasbourg was difficult so we decided to move away. I'd liked living on Île d'Yeu so I applied for a job there as a teacher, but they didn't have a post for me. I found one, however, in La Rochelle, which is a harbour town close to Île de Ré. Île de Ré is a large island, a well-known tourist attraction, much better known than Île d'Yeu at that time.

I went to La Rochelle with Laurence, who was then three years old. Because the American army was still there it was impossible to find an apartment for rent. The American military had occupied all the furnished flats. Only on Île de

Ré could I find a place for us to live. Nowadays, there is a bridge crossing to the island from the mainland but in those days you had to take the ferry. When I had found a place I called my husband to join us with our other children, Stephan and Daniel. That is how Driss always helped me, by looking after the babies. As long as the children were small, that went well. I was glad to have Stephan and Daniel with us again.

I had to go to work by boat every day. Every morning I left on a moped with a plastic coat lined with newspaper because I was so cold. I took the ferry with the early workers. Then I went to the Lycée where I was teaching. I kept formal clothes in a cupboard there to change into. It was my way of improving my confidence, by making myself look smart and elegant. After teaching I changed into my old clothes again and rode the moped back to the ferry.

It was hard on my health, and I came down with severe angina and a high fever. The doctor told me to stop working immediately, and I was given time off. A little later I was able to resign because we got some money from Driss' third or fourth book. And I got some translations to do, detective novels, stupid things, but that also provided us with some money. We stayed there for a few years.

My daughter Dominique was born on Île de Ré, in the hospital in Saint-Martin-de-Ré, in 1962. It was a wonderful birth. The hospital was very small with about four rooms, and the windows of my room were full of sunshine.

I had a special midwife who followed the principles of Dr Leboyer, the advocate of natural birth. One of his methods is to let women give birth in water. Unfortunately, this wasn't possible for me. But he had other methods that were also very good. I was the only pregnancy at the hospital then, so it was very different from giving birth in these big hospitals where you are just a number. I was very lucky: I was looked after like a princess for four days with my lovely baby.

(Dominique and I went back to that little hospital on Ile de Ré a few years ago, and they told us that she was the last baby born there. And since the bridge was built, the hospital has closed down, as people can now get to La Rochelle very quickly.)

At the time we were living in a big house in the middle of the island. Driss had to look after the three other children. We didn't have the money to pay for a babysitter, so when he came to visit me he left the children playing in the big garage. He just locked the door. There was some kind of wardrobe in the garage and I don't know what happened but the wardrobe fell over. When Driss got home he found Stephan underneath it! Happily no one was hurt.

We stayed on the island and were quite happy there until the prices started to go up. The island became more popular. A famous French actor had bought a property there and everybody came to see it. People discovered the island and started to buy houses there. So we moved back to Île d'Yeu, which was not yet so well known, and were happy again there, as ever.

Until some supposedly well-intentioned friends came and visited us, that is. I think they meant well. They were friends of mine from university but they had – how shall I put it? – taken their place in mainstream society. They were well-off and one of them had become a famous psychologist or psychoanalyst. Many friends visited us, but he came often.

He said, 'You can't go on like this. It's not fair. Your children deserve to be able to be in touch with the real world. They need a proper education and to be able to meet young people of their own age in civilised surroundings.'

The real world, mind you! And my children, of course, went to school like all children. But he went on and on, trying to convince us. Driss and I were too young and naive. My friend thought that Driss could make money in Paris and eventually he convinced us to return there.

And this, of course, was not what we should have done, although, because we did it, in another sense it was probably what we had to do. But I think it marked the end of our relationship.

I sat down and looked out over the fields through the kitchen window. The sun was going down and the light on the grass and trees was beautiful.

A big colourful apple was lying on the kitchen table. I looked at the fields and at the apple, and suddenly the Light came again.

'I don't need Driss,' I thought. 'All this is still beautiful and the same as it ever was. This apple is like a jewel, shining and beautiful. I can enjoy this whether Driss is here or not.'

The realisation was like a sudden shock and got me going again.

4
End of honeymoon

How would it be to suffer pain every day, I ask myself, sometimes to the point that turning the key in the door becomes too difficult? Why does a car accident happen, through no fault of your own, just after a difficult recovery from an operation? Why do *things like that happen?*

When I arrive the next morning I ask, 'How is the pain today, Catherine?' 'Oh, the same, pretty bad,' she laughs.

From the shadows underneath her eyes I see she must be tired. She told me that when she wakes up in the morning she immediately takes painkillers, but they take a couple of hours to work. During those hours she usually works at her computer and translates Douglas' books into French. She does it to distract her from the pain, she says, and also because she feels Douglas close by then.

When the pain is really strong she sits down with her flowers: 'Flowers are the best doctors. I sit very still and look at the flowers. Then I become the flowers.'

When the nurse has arrived to help her dress and Catherine feels a bit better, we sit down at the little kitchen table.

When we moved from Île d'Yeu back to Paris we didn't have enough money to live on. We found a cheap flat in a poor suburb. Driss was out all day, trying to find a job on the radio or television. I stayed at home with the four kids and got pregnant with the fifth one, Michel. My relationship with Driss was changing. I began to resent his attitude, that he wouldn't help me earn money to have a better life. He rarely did anything in the house. He would write and go and meet people at radio and television stations, while I had to stay at home with the kids. Our honeymoon had lasted fifteen years; now it was in peril.

I tried to take up acting in radio plays again, which only required my absence from home for a few hours. And both together with Driss and on my own, I made programmes for a radio station called France Culture, a fascinating job which I enjoyed very much.

But our relationship was slowly deteriorating. I was struggling to survive, and Driss was obsessed only with his future as a writer.

In 1964, Michel was born. He was beautiful and sweet and I adored him.

Most of the time I was left at home with the children. I was very short of money so I had no modern amenities, like a washing machine. I had to do all the washing the old way, in a boiler, including the diapers. It was a very heavy boiler and I had to lift it on to the gas stove. I injured my back and after months of pain I had to be operated on. Driss showed that he was still very good at looking after the children at times like this.

When I had recovered I looked for a job as a teacher and found one in Versailles. We were also able to get an apartment there that was reserved for government employees. It was in a suburb near a big forest, and much nicer for the children. So I began to teach again. But this time I was already trained and got a slightly higher salary. With my salary I made more money than Driss. His books still weren't selling well even though they were universally praised by the literary world.

I met many male colleagues in my job and he met many women in television and radio. All this made things worse between us.

The next year my mother died. It was one of the saddest events of my life. I loved my mother dearly. I think she put up with a lot because of me, like my staying with Garry Davis and the police coming to our house. And I'd left her to go to Paris because I wanted to be free; I wanted to become an actress and all that.

When she was old and couldn't stay on her own anymore, she went to live with my brother and his wife. They had a huge apartment and gave my mother a room as big as these two rooms together. She had a table and chairs there so she could receive people. My brother really was a lovely man.

But my mother probably wasn't very happy there. She didn't like my brother's wife very much. This lady had been my brother's secretary. She felt that, coming from a lower social level, she had now climbed up to the middle class – which was ridiculous, because a less snobbish person than my mother you couldn't imagine, and my brother was the same. But his wife had this rather unpleasant attitude.

Another thing was that my brother's wife was always sick. My brother spent his life looking after her – far more than she ever looked after him, although she made up for it when he had the ridiculous accident he eventually died from. After that she was really nice.

Also my mother wasn't very happy because I wasn't there. Whenever I came to visit her she would say, 'Apart from the times you are here no one hugs me anymore.' My brother was not demonstrative at all and his wife wasn't either. I felt guilty but what could I do? I was in Paris with my five children.

When I heard that she was going to be operated on I immediately took a train from Paris. I arrived at six o clock next morning and went straight to my brother's house. I had a shower and a cup of coffee and called the hospital to ask when I could visit. 'We allow people to come after eight,' they said. 'I'll be there at five past,' I said. It was then seven o'clock. At a quarter to eight they called me to say that she had just died.

That broke my heart. I hadn't been able to tell her for the last time how much I loved her. Everybody reassured me that she knew I loved her. But now, 50 years later, I am still sad about it. I'll never forget that I couldn't see her one last time, although I am also now profoundly aware that in infinite Reality it doesn't matter.

1968 saw the French student revolution. It was a wonderful year. It was the hippie era: make love and not war. Many young people believed that revolution would prevail. They wanted to live peacefully together and they threw out their television sets. People started to grow vegetables in the streets. Some people think the same way nowadays: they want to stop the tide of materialism and live peacefully together.

It was a happy time. We all believed life would continue in this way, but it didn't. It was not at all in the government's interests. It seemed possible at first, because the workers and the students were working together – until one day the Communist Party came to an agreement with the government. They persuaded the workers to stop demonstrating with the students, and when the students were left on their own, the revolution was finished.

For me personally, it was also a lovely time because I began to take teaching seriously. I knew that from then on I needed to be a good teacher. It was marvellous because the teenagers in my classes wanted freedom and friendship and personal responsibility. My students wanted to be independent. I taught in this way with no problem at all. I didn't need to impose any discipline. We had a wonderful time together.

Not long ago I found a photograph of one of my last classes in Versailles, which reminded me of the good times we'd had. I really enjoyed teaching at that time although, my goodness, it had not been easy to learn how to teach well. I started teaching English not only through Shakespeare and Milton but also through the Beatles and Bob Marley and recordings of Kennedy's and Martin Luther King's speeches.

A teacher in France doesn't work the whole day, which was good for my children. I could be back around four o'clock in the afternoon. The only problem was the papers I had to mark. I did that at night when they were sleeping. I started to teach the children cleaning and cooking so we could share the tasks at home. Everybody had to do his or her share. Nowadays, all my children, boys and girls, can cook, wash, iron and do DIY.

In 1969 Laval University in Quebec, Canada, offered Driss a job as a teacher of North African literature. He went there for six months. They really appreciated him and we thought about moving to Canada. I didn't want to stay in Paris while he was away so I took the children to Île d'Yeu.

When he came back I went to the airport in Paris to welcome him. I immediately felt that something was wrong. When we were back on Île d'Yeu my lung collapsed. It completely deflated and I had a pneumothorax. I felt as if I was going to die and they took me by helicopter to a hospital in Nantes.

Naturally I assumed that Driss would take care of the children. What happened next is unbelievable. Driss told Laurence he had to go back to Canada. 'Please look after your brothers and sisters,' he said to her. He took the boat and left her behind at the pier. This is how crazy he was: she was only thirteen years old. I can't understand how he could leave her like that, but there really is nothing to understand. He was like so many artists, with their total lack of consideration; totally self-concerned. All that matters for them is their creative work. Laurence was very traumatised by this event. I can still hardly believe it when I think of it.

Driss had troubles in Canada. A young student had fallen in love with him and they had had an affair. I think she got pregnant and he went back to find a solution. I don't think he intended to stay with her because, at the same time he was having this affair, he was sending me the most wonderful love letters you can imagine. I still have them here. It shows the kind of person he was.

The school teachers on Île d'Yeu each took one of my children home and looked after them. It took me a long time to recover, after I'd got back from hospital.

One day Driss phoned: 'Please come. I am in trouble.'

I flew to Quebec and took a taxi to the place he lived. His landlady let me in. He was standing in his room looking out of the window. He did not look at me. When he turned around his face was all blue. The young girl's brothers had beaten him up.

Naturally, once the scandal had emerged, his career there was over. He was accused of seducing a student. He had spent all his money. I didn't know what to do. But I still loved him and he was the father of my children. I couldn't put right what he had done. The only thing I could do was to take him away. I had enough money to pay for his ticket. So we flew back together and moved into another house in Île d'Yeu.

Even though he regretted what he had done and felt remorse, our life as a couple was difficult from then on. In a way it had been predictable that this would happen one day. Driss was handsome and charming and very intelligent. Women fell in love with him. But this was the first time that he became seriously involved outside of our marriage.

We moved back to our flat in Paris. I resumed teaching. It was a very difficult time. The children started to get angry with their father because he didn't do anything. Until they became teenagers, Driss had always helped to take care of the children. It took me some time to understand it. He could look after small children perfectly well, but when they got older, had their own problems and didn't agree with their father, it didn't work anymore. In fact, Driss himself was an eternal teenager, as many artists are. My children were not happy, neither was Driss nor I.

Then one day things really cracked. A Scottish girl had come to my school to improve her French. Her name was Sheena. She was an assistant at the Lycée, teaching English conversation. She was all alone and, for a foreigner in France, it's true, it is very difficult to make friends. I pitied her. I liked her so I invited her to my home. Then she fell in love with my husband and started to lead him on. My neighbour told me that, as soon as I left home, she would come to see him. And it was easy for him to fall for her, because we were fighting most of the time. Free love: it was the spirit of the 70s.

One day Driss disappeared. I soon understood why: he hadn't paid the rent for months. The bailiffs came to take everything away. The first time I could stop them. The second time they came I couldn't. The only things they left were the cooker, the fridge, a table, as many chairs as there were people in the home and our beds. They also took a few pieces of beautiful furniture I had inherited from my mother, furniture that had been saved from the Germans by friends during the war. We found ourselves in an empty flat.

In a way what happened was good for me because it made me rediscover who I was as a person. Not yet who I was as the big One, but at least who Catherine was as a human being and what her purpose was in life. I realised that even being attached to my mother's furniture was holding me back. Losing it set me free.

After the business with the rent, Driss came back several times. He asked me if he could come home and I said, 'Yes, provided you change your attitude and you start to help me.' I really wanted to get out of the poor neighbourhood we were living in. But Sheena kept following him around. Every time he didn't want to do the things I was asking him to do, he went back to her. Finally he just accepted her. He was afraid to tell me, but one day he said that he was going to marry Sheena. Crazily enough he had five children with her as well.

He was becoming better known and had been invited to give a big lecture at L'Institut du Monde Arabe in Paris. Several times he'd asked me if I would attend, so I had promised to be there. It was a huge event. By the time I arrived after work, the lecture had already started. The door of the venue opened right in the centre of the aisles so everybody saw me coming in. Driss was speaking. He stopped and said, 'Here is the woman who is the reason that I agreed to give this lecture.' I felt embarrassed. Our old friends began to clap while I had to walk all the way among them to my chair.

❂

When Driss and I finally parted, the children and I were left on our own. My son Daniel loved his father and couldn't understand why he had left. Unfortunately, at the same time, he was also abandoned by his girlfriend, whom he'd passionately loved. He turned to drugs. At first I didn't realise what was happening; I didn't know anything about drugs. He had been acting strangely but I hadn't realised why. When I eventually discovered that he was on heroin, it was too late: he was already addicted. I did everything I could but it was a lost battle from the start. You think they've stopped using but the next day they're on it again.

Alone with all these problems, I started to get depressed. Our kitchen window overlooked the countryside; I can still see it as if it were now. One day, when I came home from work, I sat down at the kitchen table and looked out over the fields. It was dusk. The sun was going down and the light on the grass and trees was beautiful.

A big colourful apple was lying on the table. I looked at the fields and at the apple and suddenly the Light came again. 'All this is still beautiful and the same as it ever was. I don't need Driss,' I thought. 'This apple is like a jewel, shining and beautiful. I can enjoy this whether he is here or not.' The realisation was like a sudden shock, and the Light got me going again.

Eventually the children and I got used to living on our own. And I succeeded in moving out of the cheap flat in the poor neighbourhood. It was becoming bad for my children, especially for Daniel; many young people around were turning to drugs. I found a house in the countryside further away from Paris. We rented it with two friends. We wanted to create a community to help young people. The house was beautiful, but I had to travel a long way to get to work.

Our community didn't last long. The house was too expensive: we couldn't keep up with the costs: the rent, the heating, the water and all the children. Actually, they weren't kids anymore but teenagers. They said they would help us with the bills but they couldn't find a way of making money, except for Stephan, my eldest son, who was a bit older. He was smart and courageous and decided to help me. He began to work in computers, at entry level, to help me pay for everything. This proved to be a good preparation for his future, for he has become a brilliant informatics architect.

Even though my two adult friends also brought in some money, it was all too difficult and we had to give up. Two years later, we moved back to Paris again.

Around that time I met my second great support, Kalu Rinpoche, a Buddhist teacher. Alain, a friend of my son Stephan, was practising Buddhism. One day he said, 'I see that you're not well. I want you to meet this extraordinary man who's just arrived from Tibet.' Alain was right: I was feeling depressed. Although I was not very interested in meeting this Tibetan, he took me anyway to a suburb in Paris where Rinpoche was staying with some Vietnamese people.

When we entered the house they had me sit on a sofa. Suddenly I felt bathed in pure bliss. All my problems vanished. After a while they said, 'Now you may come and meet Rinpoche.' When they took me upstairs, I realised that his room was just above the sofa where I had been sitting.

When I entered he was sitting cross-legged, as always, on his bed. He was already 70 or 80 years old by then. There was an interpreter there and he asked me, 'So what are your problems?'

'I came here full of problems but now they are all gone,' I said.

Rinpoche started to laugh and scratched his head. 'It's the Buddha, it's the Buddha!' he said.

He was a lovely, lovely man, just pure transparent light. We talked for a while. I said I couldn't be a Buddhist because I couldn't speak Tibetan. My friends who had started to practise Buddhism were reciting mantras and I couldn't understand one word.

'I feel like an actress if I pray and sing in a language I don't understand,' I said.

He answered, 'It is not important. The only thing is to see the Clear Light within.' The Buddhists' central teaching is 'the Clear Light'. Then I told him about Daniel and he said, 'I'll try to help you.' Kalu Rinpoche was the perfect vehicle for the Clear Light; you could feel the Light within him and all around. I can still feel it.

I met him several times, and every time it was wonderful. The last time I saw him he was giving what Buddhists call 'initiations' in a monastery north of Paris. It was a five-day seminar. I couldn't pay for it but they took me on as a cook. We cooked in the monastery kitchen. They had put up a big tent for Rinpoche to give his lectures in. Every time he went to the tent he passed the kitchen, and every time he passed he came to the window to say hello. And as soon as the lecture started we went to the tent to listen.

On the last day he gathered everyone together for a talk. I began to cry, I couldn't stop. I had no idea why I was crying. (Later I understood the reason: he died not long after, it was the last time I would see him alive.) He gave me an interview through an interpreter and I told him I was so sad.

'I think I cry because it is so difficult for me to see you,' I said.

He said, 'You don't have to be sad, because whatever happens to me or to you, my spirit is wide space, it is wide aware space. Your spirit is also wide aware space. In that aware wide space we will always be one.'

That is the essence of what he said to me. Of course it took me straight back to the experience I'd had when I was sixteen. For a moment I could see the Light again and feel this powerful love.

Driss died in 2007 when I was living in Nacton. It was only two months after Douglas' death and I was still in shock. I couldn't go to his funeral. Apparently it was an impressive event: the King of Morocco had recognised him as a writer and he sent his own aircraft to France to take Driss's body back to Morocco. He was buried in all pomp. His second wife and their children were there. I felt sad that I hadn't been able to see him again.

My children didn't go to the funeral either. It was too hard for us. Dominique, Stephan and Daniel had been with him when he died. Laurence, however, actually refused to go to the funeral, opposed as she was to her father. She was resentful that he hadn't made an effort to make our life easier by bringing in some money. She was also traumatised by her father's abandoning her on the pier of Île d'Yeu. Driss had acted like a self-centred patriarch, and Laurence had become a feminist. The two of them had often fought, although deep down they adored each other.

Nobody understands why I loved Driss so much. I still love him, even though I had to part from him. I know why he behaved the way he did. It's obvious that he couldn't have been different. I had fifteen happy years with him, for which I am grateful. As my wise son Michel says, 'It's a pity it couldn't go on.' It truly couldn't go on. He was driving me to total financial ruin. With five children I couldn't continue like that.

Driss taught me many things. I had been open as a child but was still a westerner from a bourgeois family. He opened my mind to Arab culture: to wonderful books like Avicenna, Averroes, Ghazali and Ibn Khaldoun. He introduced me to poetry like Rumi's and the music of Munir Bashir and Oum Khalsoum.

Our early French literature was greatly inspired by Arab literature. Our love songs were directly imported from the Arabic culture. Mathematics was an Arab invention. The cipher zero came from the Arabs, and all numbers derive from zero. Arabic architecture is beautiful. We owe them a lot, because they stand at the root of our civilisation, although I wouldn't exactly call it civilised at the moment.

All of this I discovered through Driss. We also had the same non-conformist, open-minded view of life and the world.

Driss had a lot to put up with: I think he suffered more than I realised at the time. He really was a nice person but life was hard for him. He never told me much about his childhood. I knew, however, that he came from a family with seven children. Probably he was spoilt as a child: his father thought he was the most intelligent of his children and wanted him to succeed in a great career. So he gave Driss a room for himself to study in, while the other children shared one room. His brothers and sisters were jealous and resented him.

At the age of ten he had to leave his family. His father put him in a Lycée although he couldn't speak French. This Lycée was for French children, not for Moroccan boys or girls. His father had bribed the headmaster to accept him. So Driss found himself in a French Lycée with 800 French people and three or four Moroccans. Of course he was bullied and humiliated, and in his child's mind he decided, 'One day I will speak French better than them and I will become a famous French writer.' And he did! I realise that, deep down, he was very angry. I had hoped that my love for him would get rid of his anger but it doesn't work like that, unfortunately.

Later, when I met Driss's old school friends from the Lycée, all of whom had ended up with top careers in Paris, they told me that when Driss was in his final year for the baccalauréat he became the school poet. Everybody admired him. Then his father sent him to France to become a doctor, but he didn't want to become a doctor, he wanted to write.

I know he loved me very much, he gave me lots of proof of that, but even more than me he loved writing. He needed to write. That is why I don't feel resentment towards him. And I'm glad that I supported him, for he has left a great contribution to human thinking and to world literature.

I have read about what immigrants go through when they are torn away from their culture. They are caught between two stools (if not more), which has a great impact on their identity. And it is terrible to have to submit to being despised and humiliated: it is difficult to recover from that. This is what makes the next generation of immigrants so vengeful.

People who have been colonised, like the Moroccan people, are made to believe they are inferior, just like black people in America. I remember that Martin Luther King said that his worst problem was his black brothers who still thought they were inferior. This was also true for Africans in France.

In France, when you are self-employed and need help from the national health service, you (or your employer) have to make insurance payments. Driss didn't pay so we had no insurance. When one of the children was ill I didn't know what to do. Often I noticed, during my years with Driss, that many doctors dream of being artists; they really admire them. When I told doctors that I had no insurance and no money and they heard that Driss was a writer, they would come for free.

We had a friend, a doctor and psychoanalyst, who loved Driss dearly. He spent a lot of time with him. This was the same man who persuaded us to leave Île d'Yeu and return to Paris because he thought Driss could make money there. But Driss couldn't make money in Paris, nor anywhere else! He told me that, just before he died, Driss had said that no one had really understood his work except me.

Although Driss became successful as a writer, a subject of study in many universities and of several important theses around the world, and although his books became bestsellers in Morocco, he never made a lot of money. Not many people in France were interested in his books because they deal with the problems of immigration. In fact, these are the very problems the world is facing now.

Recently I've been re-reading a few of his books. In one of his last books he wrote something terrible, as if he was speaking to his Arab compatriots: 'I am afraid now that you have no future but your past.' That's what's happening right now: some of the Arabs are going back to the middle ages! I think Driss died a sad man. He'd had so much hope that things would change, that there would be a revolution, but only now is this beginning to happen.

I don't think Driss was far from Seeing. Some sentences in his books are so full of poetry that I am sure he was close to seeing this other dimension in life. But he was too angry and too intellectually brilliant.

I don't feel resentment towards him, I will always love him. The only thing that I deeply regret is the harm he did to our children.

When something has to happen,
the whole universe works together for it to happen.

5

The man and his message

We have a break. Catherine's throat gets sore from talking after a while. She tells me that it is a result of the cold damp winters in Strasbourg when she was a young child. She caught angina every winter which eventually damaged her vocal cords.

On the balcony I straighten my legs and look at life at street level below. Some children run by screaming. The mother follows with a baby in a buggy. She calls something in French. For a moment the children halt, then they start running and yelling again. I try to imagine how Catherine managed her five.

'Would you tell me again what you told me last night?' I ask. 'The story about the lily of the valley?'

Yes, she does not mind at all and tells the story again, as vividly as if she'd never told it before.

In France we have a tradition that everyone is allowed to sell little bouquets of lily of the valley on May 1st. The flowers are supposed to bring luck and happiness to everyone. We were short of money. I had only 300 francs left for the whole month. It was almost May 1st so I decided we would try to sell lily of the valley in the streets.

We went to a wholesale market and bought plants for 300 francs. This was all the money I had left, I was taking a big risk. We spent the whole day making little bouquets. Next day we got up at three in the morning so that we could occupy a good spot in the street. (You have to be early, as everybody tries to take the best places.) We chose a good spot for my little stall and, luckily, I was not thrown out, because sometimes people fight over places.

At eight o'clock my children had to leave for school and work, and I was left by myself. By ten o'clock I realised, 'My God, I just can't sell!' Everybody else around me was selling and I had not sold a thing. I sold maybe two or three bunches over the whole day.

When my children came back at five o'clock I was almost in tears. Then a miracle happened: they took over and two hours later they had sold all our bouquets! My children are good sellers. We had doubled our money. I was lucky, I now had more than 600 francs, but what a risk it had been!

I am not a saleswoman. When I was employed as a young girl by the big department store in the States to model French dresses, they said to me after a while, 'Now you are going to sell the dresses too.' I never succeeded in selling any of them because I couldn't lie. When a large woman tried on a smart dress and was getting enthusiastic about it, I would say, 'Sorry, madame, it's not for you.' My employers gave up on me after a week.

In 1980 we moved again, to an apartment in Bois d'Arcy, a suburb of Paris. At last I had succeeded in being appointed to a college in the place we lived in, so I didn't have to drive such a long way to work anymore. It was still a difficult time for me and my children, although Laurence had already left home by then. She had fallen in love with Frederic, whom she met at the school where she worked as an assistant and who is now her husband. (In France they employ older students in schools to ensure that the children obey the rules in the corridors and other places.) Frederic was a young maths teacher there. They had gone for a long trek through the Far East and then had got married.

At that college in Bois d'Arcy I got fed up with teaching, not because of my students but because of the conservative French educational system. Most teachers in France don't want to change anything. I did creative projects with my students – for example, putting on theatre shows at the end of the year. I had the kids do everything: write the script, play the music, paint the sets. Only a few other teachers helped. This went on for three years and we held three wonderful shows. The students were happy: some of them had failed in the classroom but succeeded on stage. For those students the show enabled them to re-evaluate themselves.

During the third year I was called to a meeting with the headmaster, and he told me the shows had to stop. The other teachers found them a nuisance, he said. Sometimes I'd asked my colleagues to allow a few kids to come to my rehearsals between four and five in the afternoon rather than attend their usual class. In France they keep the kids sitting in school until five. You can imagine what they learn that last hour: nothing! Everybody knew this and still they did it. Besides, my request was always made at the end of June.

The real reason why they wanted me to stop was that the other teachers didn't want to do the extra work for the project. I, on the other hand, worked about 70 hours a week. The decision to cancel the shows made me so disgusted with the French school system that I resigned. I had to see the year out, though, before I could leave.

I decided I'd like to become a yoga teacher and try to make a living by teaching yoga. I would train in India with the famous yoga master BKS Iyengar himself, whose method I had been practising in Paris for several years. For months of training at Iyengar's Institute in Poona I would pay the same amount as I would pay in France for one weekend with his students. My children were old enough for me to leave; they had found partners or jobs. I left my apartment to Michel, who was the last one still living with me. I sold my car for enough money for me to be able to stay in India for two years, practising yoga and travelling. India was still cheap then.

Those years in India were enchanting. I lived on almost nothing, I had 200 francs a month. I went to yoga classes and I made friends. At first I stayed in a cheap lodging house for foreigners but it wasn't very comfortable. Then I made friends with an Indian woman who was attending the same yoga class. 'Why don't you come and live with us?' she said. 'I have a spare room.'

Her husband was a policeman. They were middle class and lived in a small house. On the first floor was a nice room with a terrace and a wonderful bougainvillea. Except for a small bed, the room was empty. And I had a great luxury: a shower! It was a cold shower, of course, but a shower all the same! And I had a little *rechaud* to cook on, a little camping stove, so I could make my own meals. There I lived, and the room and my food cost me so little that I had plenty of money left.

I had two Punjabi suits: a long tunic and tight trousers in a thin material. I washed them in the evening and the next morning they were dry. I had two pairs of sandals. And that was all, except for my favourite music cassettes which I had brought from home. I still listen to that music now: Bach, Mozart, Bob Marley and Ravi Shankar. And I rented a bicycle. I cycled to town for breakfast, then on to the morning yoga class and back with my friends. Then I went back to yoga in the evening.

I made a few radio programmes about India for the French radio station France Culture. I had brought with me the best little recorder you could find in France in order to interview Indian people. As soon as I met someone interesting I would interview them. Because I lived not far from Osho's ashram, I recorded the devotees singing. Osho wasn't there at the time but his followers used to sing and listen devotedly to his teachings from Oregon. These radio programmes made me some money, too.

I became friends with many women in India. Some of them didn't speak English, they only spoke Marathi. I tried to learn a bit of Marathi but it is a difficult language. Sometimes I made deep connections without talking, which was marvellous: we understood each other by just being together. I met many brave women who were already fighting for women's rights in India but, unfortunately, things were and are still bad out there.

Occasionally the Yoga Institute asked me to leave for a month because they needed my place for other westerners. Then I would travel: travelling was cheap too. Once I travelled to Nepal. The whole journey by train from Bombay to Nepal – about 5,000 or 6,000 kilometres and taking three days – cost me ten euros! I slept on the top berth of a compartment and enjoyed observing Indian life beneath. I met many people on the train.

I travelled to the Himalayas, walked to both the Annapurna and the Mount Everest base camps. I always walked with people I'd just met and become friends with.

There was a village called Langtang I walked to, about 4,000 metres up along the Chinese frontier, where I spent a few days. I saw pictures of that village two weeks ago on television. Terrible! An earthquake had completely destroyed it, and 200 people had been killed. I had met some of them.

For two wonderful years I lived in India without really owning anything. I realised you could live and be happy with almost nothing at all. I felt rich, and I didn't need more. I was extremely happy there.

At the Yoga Institute I met a dear friend, Ian Hubble, a young Englishman. Mr Iyengar held special medical classes in which he treated serious illnesses. Ian had spondylitis, a chronic condition of the spine. The doctors in London had told him that they had no cure: they couldn't do anything for him. Mr Iyengar wasn't able to provide a complete cure for Ian, but he enabled him to function normally again. He always found a way out for people with serious illnesses.

Ian and I became close friends, doing yoga together for a whole year. The day came when he had to leave, and we cycled to the beach to have a meal by the sea to mark his departure.

That night we cycled back along a country road so narrow it was impossible for vehicles to pass. A jeep drove by at high speed and forced me off the road. I fell with my bicycle into a deep ditch and broke my wrist. I was in terrible pain and couldn't move. The jeep driver didn't even stop. Fortunately, Ian was with me and helped me out of the ditch. We waited for another car to take me to the next village.

To our surprise there was a hospital in this small Indian village! They operated on me and put my wrist back in place. Not very well – my wrist is still not straight – but at least they put it back and bandaged it, which stopped the pain. I was lucky I didn't get an infection because it was just an Indian hospital in the smallest village you can imagine. The hospital staff were really nice and Ian was a darling. He stayed with me all night, even though his plane was leaving early next morning from Bombay.

After that I couldn't move my wrist anymore, it was as if paralysed. When I went back to France to get my visa renewed, I went to a doctor. He said, 'We can't do anything. We would have to break it again. You'd better get used to having a rigid wrist.'

Back in Poona at the Yoga Institute, Mr Iyengar looked at it. He said, 'No problem! I'll sort this out. I will fix it.' And he did! He showed me several points along my arm to work on and he made me work on it as he always did, with real precision and rigour. After two months I could move my wrist again.

Mr Iyengar was an extraordinary yoga master, a genius. He had no spiritual pretensions. The yoga he taught was a special kind. He knew every millimetre of the human body by heart and how everything is mutually dependent and coordinates with everything else. He told you to put your body in the right positions and to work on your body so that the energy flowed correctly. That's what the yoga postures were intended for. The spiritual aspect of yoga would appear to you later on, and you would discover your spiritual being. This was true: I found my centre thanks to him, my oneness with the world in a physical way.

Mr Iyengar himself could do any posture, he was really impressive. When you can do anything with your body it's easy for your ego to become inflated. He could easily have been proud of himself but that was not his message, and he would often joke about his own accomplishments. His message was that you should move towards your inner self.

Unfortunately, most westerners who studied with him

didn't get that. They became excellent yoga teachers who taught only how to do the most difficult postures. Yoga teachers like that have turned yoga into high-grade gymnastics. Getting into difficult postures is no better than what the Chinese and Korean circus people do: they too have extraordinary control over their bodies.

I was fortunate enough to be taught by Mr Iyengar himself: I am very grateful for that and to him. When he grew older he couldn't teach anymore but I heard that he was always practising. In collaboration with a medical doctor, he wrote a vast tome which shows all the postures and the relationships between the postures and most well-known diseases. It shows how you can cure diseases by practising certain postures. He was a vigorous man, full of integrity, just like Douglas. A genius of yoga.

One day Dominique phoned me. She was distraught. She said she hated her job as a top secretary and that her work was meaningless and only helped a few selfish people to make more money. She wanted to care for other human beings and become a nurse. So I went back to France to help her pay for her studies.

Back in Paris I found work at a company that offered ongoing training for employees. I taught English to engineers from the National Board of Electricity. I was paid well and made enough money to help Dominique through her three years of study, in which she excelled. At the end of the course, she was awarded her national degree as a nurse.

I met Douglas when she passed her last exams. It was exactly the right time – I couldn't have left Paris before!

The way the two of us met is unbelievable. Stephan had a friend, a pianist and spiritual searcher. We had long discussions together. He used to read all the classic and modern spiritual masters.

One day he came to our apartment and said, 'I've read a book and I'm sure you'll love it. You should read it as soon as possible. It's called *On Having No Head.*'

I was so busy then that I didn't even have time to buy the book.

A few days later he came back and said: 'Much better than the book, the author is actually coming to Paris next weekend. He's giving a workshop. You must come with me!'

'Forget it,' I said. 'The workshops these people give are always expensive. I can't afford it. I'm not going.'

'No no, this man isn't expensive at all. In fact he doesn't want to be paid. You just have to share the cost of the venue.'

'I'm not shopping for a guru and I don't want to go!' I said, because I really didn't feel like going.

But I went – eventually he just dragged me along!

We arrived late. When we entered the room it was very full. Douglas was doing the Single Eye experiment[1]. As soon as I heard him say, 'See that you have no limits', I thought, 'This is it!' Next we did the Pointing experiment[2], which brought me straight back to the vision I'd had when I was sixteen years old.

I fell in love with the message and with the man. Everything fell into place. When something has to happen, the whole universe works together for it to happen.

Amazingly, at the end of the workshop, Douglas was left alone on the platform, despite the number of people present. (The man who'd organised the workshop wasn't interested in Douglas' message; he was just after the money.)

---

1. See Appendix, where I refer to this as 'The Light Within' experiment – *KV*
2. See Appendix, where I refer to this as 'The See For Yourself' experiment – *KV.*

I went up to him and said, 'I think you are a genius. What you are sharing is absolutely extraordinary. Can I do anything to help?'

He said, 'Well, you seem to speak fairly good English. Would you help me get my books translated?'

I said, 'I certainly will! And what are you doing right now?'

'I don't know,' he said. 'I have the address of a hotel but I don't know where it is.'

I had my car so I offered to drive him. We had a cup of tea and talked and talked and talked. That was it. I was absolutely thrilled.

I was so thrilled, in fact, that I organised a workshop for him at my flat. I admired him because he agreed to come just for that modest gathering and asked only for his flight costs. We succeeded in collecting that. I got 32 people to come and we sat on the floor! A Franco-English friend of mine was the interpreter. It was a real success.

Not long after that, Douglas called me from England and said, 'I'm giving another workshop in France, in Dijon. The man who was supposed to be my interpreter can't come. No one speaks English in Dijon and I'm on my own. Could you come and help by being my translator?'

This was something I'd never done before. It was difficult to take a day off work but I persuaded my employers to let me go for that Friday. From the beginning Douglas and I worked together as one. With his wonderful voice he spoke slowly and articulated the words well; it was easy to translate. After the workshop we went back to Paris together by train, where he was staying with some friends.

Two days later he was about to leave for the States. He was travelling with a plastic bag with some tools for the workshops and a few clothes like pyjamas and socks, almost nothing! Early the next morning I went to a department store and bought him a bag with wheels. I went to his friends' place.

'I bought this for you to take to the States. It's better than a plastic bag,' I said.

He found this very funny. But later he wrote to me from the States: 'Yes, it's better with the trolley!' I was delighted to receive his letters.

When he was back in England, he said that he was giving a workshop there and asked if I wanted to come along, but I had already enrolled for a big yoga seminar on the same dates. Then he invited me to a seminar in France. I said yes, of course. There we really got together. We worked together so well with the group. We were always talking to each other.

He asked if I would come to Nacton in September so that he could show me his house and his books. I said, 'Okay!'

So I went to Nacton and thereafter practically never left. We accepted that we were in love, and it was wonderful.

I went back to Paris just to give up my apartment. That was easy. I had little furniture and a friend of mine offered to store it in a garage. I left everything else and returned to Nacton with three suitcases and my record player. I've always lived with music and was afraid Douglas wouldn't have anything to play records on, although it turned out that he did.

That's how it all started. The two of us meeting was a miracle for both of us.

Catherine's parents

1942, Catherine's father Albert Birckel just before he died

1933, baby Catherine

1939, seven years old just before the war

1946, with Zaza the big dog, Lynton, UK, at the au pair *job*

1950, North Carolina, USA, Catherine left

Catherine, left, modelling French dresses in American newspaper

With Driss in Ile d'Yeu

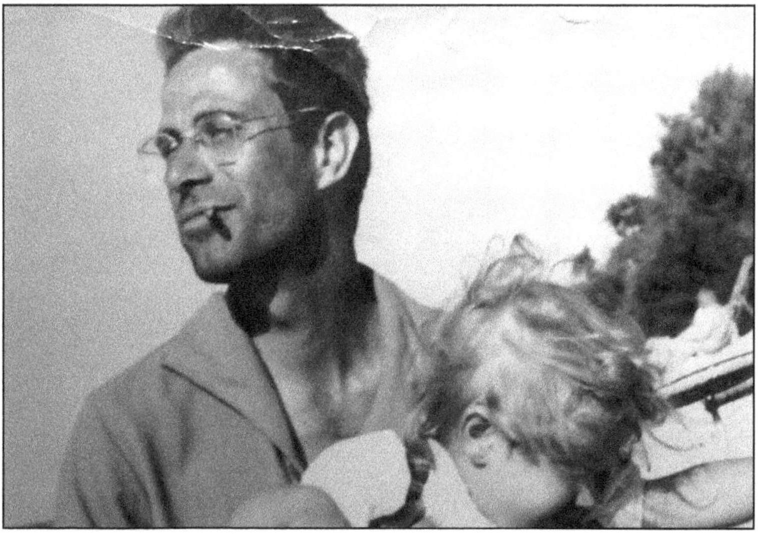

1958, Driss and baby Laurence in Ile d'Yeu

Left: *1961, with Laurence and Stephan in the Vosges*

Below: *1964, Catherine*

Facing page: upper - *1966, the five children in Ile d'Yeu*

Facing page: bottom - *1966, with Laurence, Dominique, Daniel and Michel in Versailles*

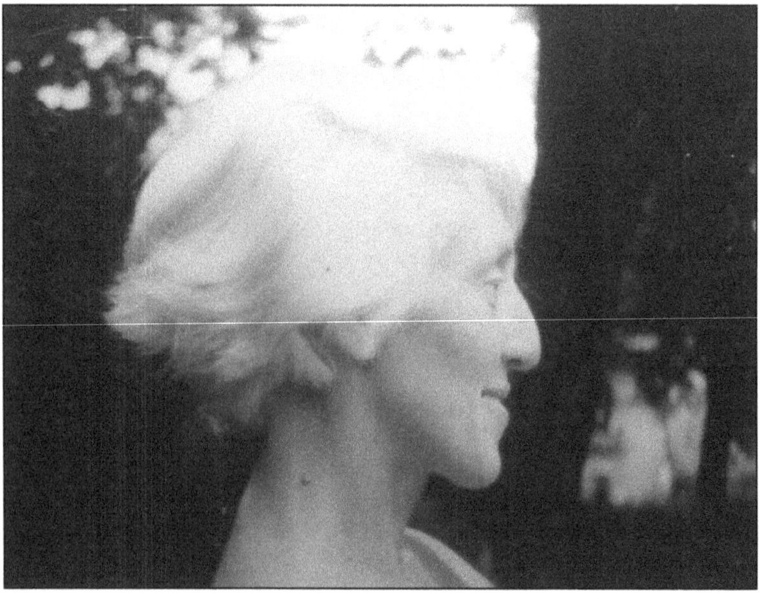

Above: *Kalu Rinpoche*
Below: *1985, Poona, India, Catherine right*

Above: *1985, on the track to the Annapurna basecamp, India*
Below: *1991, Paris, with Douglas*

Above and below: *1992, with Douglas in Le Taillé*

Above: *at Yvan Amar Centre, Hiroshima, Japan*

Below: *at a workshop in Japan*

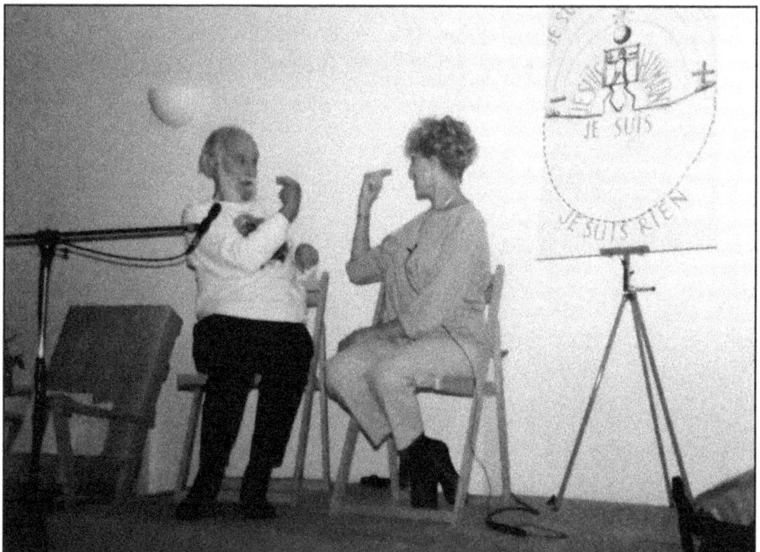

Left: *1994, at Alain Bayod's Centre in the Ardennes*

Below: *1995, at a workshop in Le Taillé*

Above: *1995, at a workshop in Le Taillé*

Right: *1999, Douglas' 90th birthday party*

Above: *1999, Douglas' 90th birthday party*
Below: *2002, Catherine's children at her 70th birthday*

2007, Douglas' Headstone at his grave in Nacton

Above: *2013, at a workshop in the Ardèche: the experience of immenseness*

Below: *2015, with Karin in France*

Above: *2015, with Karin at the kitchen table in Montpellier*

From the very moment I met Douglas it was just bliss.

I felt as if I had been sailing a boat, sailing on the ocean of life, looking for the harbour.

Meeting Douglas was like suddenly reaching my harbour.

6

Two within the One

We stand at the balcony and look out over Montpellier. It is noon. The air shimmers over the city. It is always hot and sunny here at the coast, she told me, due to the special wind, the mistral. Here the clouds have no chance. That is why many people like to retire here.

While we stand there staring over Montpellier I think about everything she has told me, both while I was recording and while I wasn't.

'From what I understand your children were not very happy with Douglas,' I ponder aloud. 'They didn't like him much and they weren't interested in Seeing. Maybe also they didn't like to see their mother leaving for England?'

'Well,' she says, 'I said to my children that I have a right to live this love.'

When I entered Douglas' house, Shollond Hill, for the first time that September, I felt immediately that it was my house, as if I knew the house already. As if I had always known it. It was a dream of a house. Douglas could have been a famous architect. His ideas on architecture were marvellous; he wanted to unite people and nature. The house opened out on to a big lawn. When all the windows were open its space was limitless: outside and inside were one. Not only was this house beautiful, it was practical too, just like Seeing. I'm translating a Swedish workshop into French at the moment, and Douglas keeps saying, 'Seeing is practical, you can use it your whole life. At any minute you can decide to look in!' His house was like Seeing, and I felt so good there.

It is such a pity that this beautiful place has been destroyed now by greedy contractors. But Douglas always used to say, 'Things are perishable – just let them go.'

That's been my view too. Before inheriting Douglas' house I never owned anything. Even now I don't have a sense of property. This apartment here and my house up in the Cévennes are for all my friends; to feel that they are just mine is ridiculous.

Our life together in Nacton began to organise itself. We got along so well. Many friends visited us. Sometimes we had a lot of people staying with us, like at Douglas' 90th birthday party. On such occasions people pitched their tents in the little woods that surrounded the house. The only thing we had to do was to hire two portable toilets because our toilets couldn't cope with that many people.

I was a very good cook then. Sometimes Douglas laughed and said, 'People don't come to see me anymore. Now they just want to have a good French meal.' We laughed a lot. One of Douglas' qualities that I really appreciated was his humour.

Most of these so-called spiritual teachers are so solemn, but Douglas used to say, 'God is full of humour. It's only the devil who is solemn.' It's true, and in French the word *humour* is close to the word *amour* or love. I don't know if this is accurate etymologically, but it's a nice connection.

We used to go on walks; Douglas was still walking at that time. Although he was 22 years older, I never felt the difference in age. His mind was still young. He was interested in everything. I sometimes forgot that his body was older. When I took him on long walks he would say, 'Catherine, this is too much! You've got me walking the long way again right along the River Orwell.' It was allowable for him to be a little more tired than I was. I was 60 and still fit, but he was 82.

I loved him very much and that is what he needed. I think he had never been loved for himself. From what I was told, his mother didn't know how to love him. He told me how badly she had treated him. As an example, one day when he was small, they were walking in Ipswich and met one of his mother's friends. This lady said to his mother, 'What a nice handsome young boy you have!' When she left his mother said, 'I hope you know that you are not handsome at all.' It touched me deeply that this kind of thing had happened often in his childhood. Nothing he did ever pleased his mother.

From what I understood, he had never really been loved for himself, as a human being, but rather as a spiritual guide. I cared so much for the man he was, I would have done anything for him. I think it was good for him. People told me that, before he'd met me, he was tired and didn't want to go on. Life was too much for him. I used to hear that, especially in America. Douglas had told his American friends that he wouldn't come back anymore; they had thought they would never see him again. They told me that the two of us meeting had given him a new lease of life and enabled him to carry on for another ten years!

At home in Nacton I translated his books into French, and Douglas carried on writing. The first I translated was *Head Off Stress*. I found out that I could do it fairly easily, although it was a lot of work as the book was so long.

I soon discovered an impressive application of Seeing. If I was translating with the idea that little Catherine was doing the job, it was difficult. But if I started working from who I really am, I disappeared and the work went flying along!

I recently discovered an extraordinary French poet. His name is Jacques Goorma and he could be Douglas' reincarnation, although he isn't because he's already 60. What is extraordinary is that he speaks the same language, sometimes word for word, without having ever met Douglas or read anything by him. I was immediately bowled over by his writings, and still am so.

The way I discovered this poet is very strange. When I opened one of his books in a bookshop, I saw that the publisher was located in Alsace, where I was born. Their publishing house is near Le Lac Noir, the Black Lake, in a village called Orbey that was very near my mother's house in the Vosges. When I was a little girl, before the war, my father took us on walks to Orbey to get Munster cheese from a special cheese-maker who lived there. We walked through the forests and on the way back we went swimming in the Black Lake.

The book I picked up was called *La Conversion*, and this is the poem I happened upon:

If in your head
You turn round
Face to no face
You see
God

He deletes you
Nothing else

You can imagine the shock! A poet who wrote like Douglas and published his work in the place where I was born! I thought it was a miracle.

One of Jacques' books is in French called *Le Séjour*. His term for who we really are is 'The Sojourn', which can mean a living room but also has a much wider meaning than that. It is our dwelling, our Home. It includes within it the word *jour*, which can mean daylight. So *Le Séjour* contains the ideas of immensity and light. I have translated it as 'The Land of Clear Light'; I can't think of a better way of putting it.

Just like Douglas, Jacques writes that being in this 'sojourn' can only happen in our absence. He says that, although I am myself this *séjour*, this Home, I need a suit in order to appear. The suit has its uses, but I am not the suit. I don't have to limit myself to my suit because this *séjour* is limitless. It is the immense awareness itself.

The French text is beautiful but difficult to translate, because Jacques creates words just as Douglas did. In French words are often more abstract than in English. The English language is more concrete. In English the poem would read like this:

The land of clear light only appears in my absence.
Nobody is there to enjoy it. And yet, it is nothing but joy.
The land of clear light only appears in my absence, and yet
I am this land, and not that person in a suit hosting an event.
A suit is useful to be seen, but it is useless to be limited
to its seams. The land of clear light is behind.
The silent light of awareness.

Douglas and I started to hold many workshops together. We conducted fifteen or sixteen a year, more than one a month. Strangely, we didn't give many workshops in England but in France we gave a lot, all over the country: in Paris, Strasbourg, Saint-Étienne, Romain, Valence.

We had a wonderful friend in France, Alain Bayod, who had been a spiritual seeker all his life. A strange coincidence was that Alain Bayod's first master had been my yoga master, Mr Iyengar. In France Alain had been working with a French spiritual teacher, Arnaud Desjardins, and he had never really found 'this', our Centre. He told me that he was desperate. He was a teacher now himself, and he felt he was a fake because he himself didn't see what he was talking about. Then someone who loved Douglas and Seeing persuaded Alain to invite us to give a workshop.

Nothing much happened for him on the first day. The second day we did the Tube experiment[3]. Afterwards Alain said that it had been like an atomic bomb! At last he had found what he had been looking for. He decided to teach Seeing from then on, but he lost almost all of his so-called disciples. They preferred the teachings of his previous master which involved a long and slow process.

Arnaud Desjardins was a very successful man who used to be a journalist. He was the first journalist to take photographs of the Tibetan masters and introduce them to France; he became famous for that. He had a master in India, Swami Prajnanpad, and he taught more or less according to Swami Prajnanpad's teachings, although not exactly. He used to interpret the doctrines in accordance with his own Christian ideas. I've read some of Swami Prajnanpad's books myself: he does talk about our Centre, although not as clearly and directly as Douglas did.

Desjardins didn't like Douglas. Douglas said that Seeing

3. See Appendix.

was easy, while Desjardins taught that it was difficult. He also said that Douglas talked too much. Once he invited us to his ashram. Douglas more or less insisted he let us give a workshop. Desjardins attended the workshop too. The only thing he said afterwards was: 'It is interesting that Douglas Harding has found ways of perceiving something that is difficult to describe.'

Desjardins had great influence in France. There is a kind of inner circle here of so-called spiritual people all affiliated to some tradition or other, and Desjardins was one of them. It is not easy to be accepted by them, especially when you have no formal traditional master and you don't belong to a lineage.

We gave workshops in Germany, in Frankfurt and Hamburg. In Frankfurt we had a strange experience. There was a guru who had a kind of new age centre. It was a big house with a huge attic which had been turned into a meditation room, where our workshop was to take place. They had spread mattresses all over the floor. For Douglas especially, but for me too, they had arranged chairs.

When we entered the room a few couples were lying on the mattresses and were virtually making love. Douglas started the workshop anyway, and the couples straightened up. But soon they started kissing and caressing again.

Douglas said, 'Look, either you make love or you attend my workshop. You have to choose because I'm not going to go on like this.'

They were nice people and things ended well. I think they were Osho people.

Every summer we visited the States for almost two months. We were often invited by a meditation group in a community in the north-east – until the invitations suddenly stopped. Their new leader forbade them to invite anyone who didn't have traditional Zen training. You needed a certificate! The same thing happened at Barre, Massachusetts, at the Insight Meditation Society's Retreat Center, a beautiful monastery in the countryside which we used to visit.

In California Douglas and I were invited to Marin County, a posh suburb of San Francisco. There was a meditation centre there – for rich people, of course. It was a wonderful place. At least 150 people came: a full house of people who were all interested in Seeing. We were introduced as Douglas and Catherine and the workshop went very well.

In this kind of place the people don't usually pay; instead they give donations. Someone holds a basket when they leave and they put money into it. In amongst the money an envelope was discovered with my name on it. When I opened it I found a lovely crystal heart (which I still have) and a piece of paper with a handwritten quotation:

> *'We live in illusion and the appearance of things. There is a reality. We are that reality. When you understand this you will see you are nothing. And, being nothing, you are everything.'*

The quotation was signed 'Kalu Rinpoche'.

It was strange because Kalu Rinpoche had died by then. Who could have known about my connection with him? I didn't know anyone in the audience. I was deeply moved, because to me it was like a message from beyond, from Rinpoche to me, which said, 'Catherine, you are exactly where you should be with Douglas!' Because Douglas spoke essentially the same language as Rinpoche had.

The note is still a mystery; I'll never know who gave it to me. But whoever that person was, we are one in the big One.

Douglas, however, would not have used the word 'illusion': he preferred to use 'impermanence'. This life is impermanent – so don't get attached to things. All that is out there is objects and they will all disappear. The only thing that never ever changes is the land of everlasting clarity.

Personally I don't like to say that here at Centre I am an empty void, because in my experience it is not void. For me the bottom of the bottom of the bottom of our origin is still presence, presence of energy. It is a vibrating energy, a silence that vibrates in such a way that it is like music. It supports me. I think it is the origin of everything, of creation itself. It is true love because, in fact, creation is an action of love.

We went to Chicago and twice to New York. We went to Seattle and down the coast to Santa Barbara and San Francisco. Very often we were in Los Angeles, where one of Douglas' closest female friends, Virginia Parsell, a real darling, organised our workshops. We also went to Hawaii, to Florida and to the end of the west coast, to San Diego; a publishing house there published some of Douglas' books. And we went to this crazy city in Arizona, Sedona, this incredible city with all these new age people and their gurus. I felt sad to see that this wonderful place with its huge impressive red cliffs that had once been a sacred site for the American Indians had now been transformed into a typical American scene, with well-trimmed foliage and little houses with well-mowed lawns.

We went to Canada, to Vancouver and several times to Quebec and Montreal. They really loved Douglas there. Their response to Douglas' death was more emotional than anywhere else in the world. They sent me the most moving messages, saying that they'd been waiting for him to come back and had really hoped that he would return.

We went to Israel three or four times, an interesting place. We were invited to an experimental village where Palestinians and Israelis lived successfully together. (This was before the first *intifada*.) We held a workshop there, and after the Tube experiment[4], a man stood up and said, 'All of this is obvious, of course. To us, here, that's to say. We are ready to see it, but we are not the people you should be talking to. You should go to Arafat and Sharon. They are the ones to do the Tube with.'

'Yes,' I said, 'but you invited us and they didn't!'

I have a lovely friend in Israel who's like a brother to me, Yossi Morgenstern, a doctor of Chinese medicine. He has a clinic in Tel Aviv. He speaks fluent French because he was born and brought up in France. The year before Douglas died he regularly came to Nacton to give him a massage. Now he does the same for me. Since he heard I wasn't well, he has already come twice to Montpellier. He is extraordinary. One evening he gave me a massage from my toes to my neck and, believe it or not, the next morning the pain was gone. That didn't last long but for two days I had no pain! He is a dedicated seer too and tries to share Seeing in his country, holding Seeing workshops.

We went to Japan three times. In Tokyo we held a workshop with about 150 Japanese people. The same thing happened there as happened to my friend Alain. After the Tube experiment a Zen monk, a gentleman with a noble appearance and dressed all in white, stood up and said, 'Thank you, Douglas. For thirty years I've been looking in vain for who I really am. And now, through your experiments, it is so clear to me. Thank

4. See Appendix.

you so much!' Tears were running down his cheeks.

He lived in a monastery and he asked Douglas, 'Can I share your experiments with my friends in my community?'

'Of course you can,' said Douglas.

Then the monk asked, 'Is there a patent? Do we have to pay something?'

Douglas said that of course he didn't need to pay anything. Then all the Japanese clapped, because apparently in Japan you never get anything without paying for it.

Japan was a revelation for me, because I had thought that Japanese people were very reserved and poker-faced. But they were not like that at all. When we gave workshops in Japan the people were so moved that they were weeping. Once, at the end of a workshop, all of them came up and embraced us, and – I swear it's true – Douglas and I ended up with wet T-shirts.

We did not go to India. Douglas had hoped that somebody would invite us there. Someone had said that they would invite us to New Delhi but they never did. Douglas had the impression that India was not yet ready for this kind of spirituality. In India they are still too much into worshipping.

We also gave several workshops in Switzerland. And, of course, we held regular Seeing workshops in our own house in Nacton.

Douglas and I had not married. I never thought of getting married, I thought that at our age it wasn't necessary. Then one night, when we were in the Ardèche, Douglas woke up and said, 'I want to marry you. Let's get married!'

Officially he was still married to his first wife. More than twenty years after they'd separated he had to ask her for a divorce. She didn't like it.

But eventually the divorce came through and we could marry. We had just a small ceremony with two witnesses, Bill and Anne. At the end the officiant said, 'Now you may kiss.' So we did. Then he said, 'Don't you even have a photographer?'

In fact, because of our travels around the world, it was better to be married. Everybody had been calling me 'Mrs Harding' when I wasn't Mrs Harding. I don't suppose Douglas liked that.

So this was our life. Of course it wasn't perfect bliss all the time because we were human beings. There were a few 'ding-dongs', squabbles rather than fights. He would have preferred me without children, for one thing! Which was difficult for me, although he loved my daughter Dominique and she loved him. Another source of friction was that he was tremendously keen on being ready at least two hours before we had to leave. He never wanted to be late, whereas I tend to leave things till the last minute. I did get impatient with that.

Then Winchester happened. We were giving a workshop at the University, which is strangely constructed, half up and half down a hill. We had to go to the cafeteria for lunch, which was at least a hundred steps up. By that time Douglas already always used to hold my arm as we walked.

After lunch we were having coffee. It was a quarter to two. Suddenly Douglas stood up and said that we had to go back down, because it was nearly two o'clock and he didn't want to be late.

I said, 'Let me at least finish my coffee. Look, all the participants are still here.'

'No, no,' he said, 'we must go!' and he refused to wait for me. He was very stubborn; he needed to be stubborn in order to accomplish everything he did. So he went down on his own and fell.

He broke his left femur and was in great pain. He was taken to the hospital and had to have an operation. He was in hospital in Winchester for months; they wouldn't transfer him to the hospital in Ipswich. All this time I was staying in student accommodation at the University. I walked all over Winchester and in the end I knew it by heart. But Douglas healed well: he was able to walk again, but from then on always with a stick.

Then the other accident happened ... Every two years I would take our car back to France to buy a new one. I had a friend who worked at the Renault factory who could arrange a discount. So for just a little more money I could buy a better car. (That's how I got to be able to afford an automatic car, although they are more expensive.) My friend had a new car ready for us and I had to go to France and pick it up.

I told Douglas that I would ask Judy Bruce, a dear and close friend in Seeing, to come and look after him. He got angry.

'No way! I don't want a babysitter. I can be on my own. If you arrange a babysitter I'll divorce you!'

So I didn't ask Judy and went off to Paris. I promised to call him every morning and evening.

One day I called and nobody answered the phone. Immediately I rang Ipswich Hospital and asked if they had a patient called Douglas Harding. 'Yes,' they said, 'Mr Harding was admitted yesterday.' Douglas was 92 then.

This time the damage was worse than before. He had tripped over his stick; sticks can be very dangerous. He told me that the phone had been ringing and that he wanted to reach it before it rang off. The phone was at the other end of the living room, so he was rushing towards it with his stick and he tripped over it. He fell in the middle of the room and was too weak to get up. He couldn't reach the phone. He was about to pee in his trousers when suddenly the doorbell rang. At the top of his voice he shouted, 'Come in, come in!' Our door was never locked.

Two Jehovah's Witnesses came in and asked for Catherine. He called out, 'She is not here but I am. Could you please help me?'

They called the ambulance and he was taken to hospital. It was a complete coincidence that the Jehovah's Witnesses had arrived: they had been looking for me because they needed someone who could speak French.

I couldn't come back to Nacton straight away: I had to wait till our car was sold. But Douglas was safe in hospital.

From then on he got worse. His leg wasn't just broken: from what I understood he had twisted everything along the whole length of it. He spent a long time in hospital, and when he came out he couldn't walk by himself anymore. He was in a wheelchair most of the time. For half an hour each day we had to walk with him on a flat stretch of lane near the house. 'Walking the dog,' he called it!

At first I walked him on my own. Then my shoulder was hurt, because he was quite heavy. I tried to find some professional help but it was ridiculously expensive. Finally I became so desperate that I hung a note in the village shop.

One day somebody rang our doorbell. There was this charming lady standing there, saying, 'I've heard you're looking for help to walk your husband? I'll help you if you like.'

This was Ann Jackson, who had been a nurse. She lived in Nacton and became my best friend. She helped me with Douglas till the end. She isn't a Seeing friend: she is simply a lady who helps everyone. I think she is a natural Seer. When she was young her mother told her, 'Do to others what you would like to be done to you, and never do to them what you wouldn't like to be done to you.' That had become her rule in life. She really does to others what she would like to be done to her. I hope that someone will do the same for her when she needs it.

During the following years, Douglas still conducted workshops from his wheelchair, in England, France, Switzerland. We also went to Cyprus with the wheelchair. His last workshop was in Paris, in 2006; about 150 people were there. One could sense that it was probably the last one, and some friends were moved to tears.

He also went to the summer gatherings in Salisbury; he missed only one gathering, when he was in hospital in Winchester.

His energy was such that he could still do his drawings. He would stand up and go to the easel. I really admired his skill: even at the age of 96, he could draw a huge perfect circle in a fraction of a second. But I also began to understand that when you can't walk anymore, you slowly go downhill. If you want to stay alive, you must try to walk as long as you can.

It wasn't possible for me to do everything at Shollond Hill on my own anymore. We had a big garden, and repairs were always needed. We got some help: I had a cleaning lady, who was quite temperamental. She would turn up, or not, and she would get angry at me for no reason at all. I couldn't rely on her.

It was difficult to find professional help with caring for Douglas. I called all over the city to every agency I could find, but no one wanted to come to Nacton. It was too far, they said. By the time I called the last number I was in tears. A lady answered, 'I can tell you're desperate, so try this number.' I called the number and got another lady, Mavis, who – miracle! – said she would come immediately. She was just starting a caring agency. She was very efficient, and from that time on things went better. Mavis saved my life.

Slowly Douglas got worse, though if he hadn't fallen I think he could easily have lived to 110. Just before Christmas he came down with a kind of bronchitis with a high fever. I took him to hospital. There he told the doctor that he didn't want to be treated anymore, and that he wanted to go. The doctor respected his wishes.

Douglas told me that he would like to spend Christmas at home. I asked the doctor and he agreed, so we had Christmas at home. He deteriorated more and more. Judy came to be with us. A few French friends came. My daughter Dominique came. Richard Lang and his twin brother David came, both long-term Seeing friends. Huguette, a French nurse and a dear friend, came. I felt well supported, with all these good friends around.

It took about ten days. Douglas wasn't eating anymore. The last days I spent every night beside him in a reclining chair Mavis had lent me. It could be turned almost into a bed and I could stretch out my legs and even sleep. Douglas was in his bed and my chair was right beside it. We were side by side, holding hands, and every two or three minutes he would squeeze my hand.

Douglas had always been quite apprehensive about dying, probably because of the hell-fire sermons of his childhood.

He said to me, 'Please stay with me, stay with me until the end.'

I had promised that I would stay till the very end, but I started to cry, I couldn't help it. It was so hard to see him going.

He said, 'Let me go, let me go.'

I said, 'Yes, I'll let you go, but I can't help being so sad.'

He said some wonderful things. To me he said, 'I love you supremely. Never forget it.' When Judy said to him, 'I will miss you', he said to her, 'I will wait for you'. To David he said, 'It's very interesting, dying.'

One day, in the middle of the night, I eventually fell asleep. I was so tired; I had been up practically all day. When I woke up, I didn't feel his hand squeezing mine anymore. Judy was in the room. She said, 'Catherine, I think he's gone.' It was about two o'clock in the morning. Some say that people will wait till you are asleep or out of the room to die.

Douglas died peacefully on January 11th, 2007. I really think he did die peacefully. His face was quite relaxed. So that was it.

We are silent for a while. Then I realise that she has hardly said anything about the way the two of them were, together.

'How did you relate to each other in daily life?' I ask. 'It's not common for two people who both See who they really are to live that together, as a couple.'

'Well,' she says after a pause …

What was so good in our relationship was that in my Centre I recognised him and in his Centre he recognised me. That is why we were so close; we were always one.

Of course, each of us had our own conditioning. He was conditioned by his narrow Christian upbringing, and I was conditioned by my free non-religious upbringing. Sometimes we disagreed about some subjects. But whenever we noticed that we were back into our little selves and that we were confronting each other, we immediately realised that this was ridiculous. It didn't last for more than a few seconds, and straight away we went back into who we really are. We could never quarrel for long, although it did happen; I didn't always agree with him. Douglas used to say, 'Catherine is free: she isn't a yes-woman.' I would give my opinion and he would accept it, as I would accept his.

When I related to him I related to God within him. I know it was the same for him. As a little one[5] I disappeared for him, and he disappeared for me. Our relationship was mainly within the One, the One that we all are. We hardly needed to talk about it or to express it. It just was.

During the last years we would just sit together for long periods of time. When I finished my work I would sit next to him; he would take my hand. We didn't have to talk. We would sit on the terrace and look out, just being together. Each of us was the world. And we were the world together: the trees, the ground, the church, the sky, the birds, the deer, everything. And we were the Space for them. We just were, and the world was. We accepted our limitations caused by our different conditionings. It was total acceptance and total union: loving acceptance of each other as little ones, and all the time union as the big One. It was a marvellous relationship.

---

5. In Douglas Harding's terminology, 'the little one' stands for the little person, the little self, the conditioned personality – life experience at the human level. It is in contrast with what he calls 'the big One': our real nature here at Centre, our absolute reality. In other words, 'the little one' is a term of endearment that acknowledges the human experience of thoughts, feelings and sensations which are taking place in the infinite space that we are, here at Centre.

I thought that, with Seeing, it would be easier –
but it wasn't.

At least not at first.

7
The place of love and loss

When I enter her apartment the next morning, her home suddenly feels familiar; it has become my home too. Catherine sits at her desk. Above it hangs a picture of her and Douglas: her cheek rests against his shoulder; he looks ahead and she looks at him. They are both laughing and looking happy. There is another picture in the living room in the same happy pose: he looks outwards and she looks at him.

I notice that something has changed over the past few days: we have become friends. The generation gap between us has fallen away. Her life could have been mine had I been born in her place. When I tell her this, she nods, and says we are like sisters, sisters in Seeing.

We have breakfast. We talk and then we are silent. When we are finished, I clear the table.

'Douglas just died,' I say …

I felt half of myself had been amputated. It was very, very hard. I thought that, with Seeing, it would be easier – but it wasn't. At least not at first.

Douglas' body was taken away by the *pompes funèbres*, the people who deal with dead bodies. It was terribly hard to see him being taken away. His body was kept on their premises for a few days, until it was time for him to be cremated. We had to wait.

I went to see him there a few times before everyone else was allowed to go. I talked to him. It was good to be able to talk to him, although he wasn't in his body anymore. But one hopes that he could still hear. The Buddhists say that you are still around for a few days. I don't know if that's true but it's probably helpful psychologically for those who are left behind, to talk to the one who has gone, even if he can't hear you.

Douglas' funeral was like a dream. At the same time I knew I wasn't dreaming, and that I had to play my part. The way they do these ceremonies at crematoriums made it particularly hard. We were sitting here. The coffin was there. A few people spoke. Then suddenly a door opened and the coffin slid into a blazing furnace. You could see the fire and the coffin going into it. It's quite dramatic.

The church ceremony, however, was good. About a hundred people came and the church was full. Alan Rowland, one of our best friends and a musician, played the piano. He played all the pieces Douglas liked. People 'bore witness' as they call it. They said what they had to say about Douglas and their relationship with him. Richard Lang talked about Douglas' life.

I played my own part. I wrote the following, and read it aloud:

> *'I thank God for having granted me the privilege of being your wife. You have been, you are and will always be my beloved husband. My love for you is boundless. You've left*

your body but Here, in my heart, we are one more than ever, and for ever and ever.

'Our dear American friend George used to say about you: "He is a hell of a guy!" Yes, you were a hell of a guy! Noble, brilliant, utterly dedicated to your "mission" of sharing your spiritual experience, humorous and with such incomparable integrity!

'Perhaps what I admire you most for is that in spite of your genius you've never tried to have power over others and never thought of yourself as better than or superior to anyone.

'During the last week of your human life, your message to me was "trust, trust, trust". And the writings on the wall that you've left shining for me and for everyone are: "If your eye be single, your whole body shall be full of light, leaving no place dark." And above all: "Self-giving love is the power behind the world."

'Thank you, Douglas, for what you have shared with me and with thousands of friends throughout the world. Thank you for the heritage you've left us, the priceless pearl, the treasure, the ultimate liberation: the vision of who we really really really are.

'"Now cracks a noble heart. Good night, sweet prince, and flights of angels sing thee to thy rest."'

Judy read aloud the funeral words Douglas had written in *The Little Book of Life and Death*. Then there were a few pieces of music that Douglas loved. That's all. We didn't have any religious rituals at all.

After the ceremony we went to the house. I felt strange, like being in a cloud. It seemed unreal. About fifty people were in the living room, some standing and some sitting on the floor. All of us felt as one, in the same soul, united in our admiration of Douglas. It was very moving.

Straight away I had many problems. Dealing with them probably helped me to get over my grief. I had always known that this was going to happen. I had tried to prepare myself, but you're never really prepared when it actually happens. It was a shock that I would never see Douglas again, even though I knew that at my Centre he was with me and that he always will be.

I received a letter from his former wife, saying that I had to leave Shollond Hill. In his will Douglas had left the house to her because they had co-owned it. I had hoped that I could stay in the house, but she wrote to me that she wanted to sell and that I had to get out by July 1st. She succeeded in selling it just before the financial crisis, and for a good price too.

At that time I still thought that things would carry on in Nacton, and that perhaps the town would become famous because of its association with Douglas. I wanted him to have a headstone in the cemetery there so that he would be remembered. I had a nice headstone made and asked everyone to help with its cost.

In his will Douglas had left me Under Shollond, his other house which he had built to receive the people who were interested in Seeing after having heard his lectures in London or reading his first book, *On Having No Head*. His wife hadn't wanted to receive people in their main house, and eventually she'd left him.

But when the time came for me to leave Shollond Hill,

Under Shollond was occupied by a former wife of my friend Bill, who didn't want to move. For years she had rented the house from Douglas for a very low rent. Eventually I had to sue her, which I didn't want to do. After I had spent around £10,000 on legal fees, it was agreed that she had to go, because it was obvious that I was the owner and I was out on the street. She didn't leave the house in a good state, though. My children Dominique and Daniel came over from France and helped me to clean and paint it. As ever, they were marvellous.

What has always saved me in my life is crying. When I'm very sad, this body of mine reacts by crying. Weeping makes you surrender, give up. That year I wept for I don't know how many hours, in my bed and everywhere else.

My children came, my friends came, and slowly I got used to not seeing Douglas every minute anymore. My good friend Ann Jackson, who at first was the only person to have helped me with walking Douglas, took me for walks. She is a charming and lively woman, and a great walker. We would walk and laugh which was good for me.

I had three shocks that year: Douglas died on January 11th; my children's father Driss died on April 1st; and on August 15th my brother died.

My brother's story is sad. Twenty years previously he'd had a terrible accident. He'd gone to attend the baptism of his grandchild in Antibes on the French Riviera, where his eldest son, the baby's father, lived. After the ceremony he went back to his hotel. It was uphill and he had to climb a few steps to the door. He was carrying one of those man's bags over his shoulder. While he was walking up the steps, some scoundrel came up from behind him and grabbed the bag. My brother fell backwards down the steps, while this guy ran off. My brother fell into a coma. He later told me that there'd been 30 francs in the bag: that was all.

He was in a coma for two months, and when he woke up he was paralysed, he couldn't do anything. He could speak and he could recognise people but he couldn't walk or go to the loo. He was totally dependent on others. He never recovered and remained in hospital till the end of his life.

During the first years he was in hospital in Strasbourg. Then his second son, who lived in Toulouse, found him a place in a retirement home which also catered for the disabled.

My brother's wife was very good. He had always looked after her when they were younger, and now she looked after him, till the very end, about twenty years later.

I didn't understand why this had to happen to my brother. But now I realise that there is nothing to understand. Douglas and I talked about it a lot. He said, 'Justice does not exist. There is no justice in the universe. In the universe things happen all the time but they don't happen through any consideration of equality or justice. They just happen.'

It's true. For plants and animals there is always conflict in their struggle for survival. A drought comes and both plants and animals die. There is rain or a tsunami or a bad storm and also people die. There is no justice. Why does one suffer more than another?

One day, after a long discussion, Douglas concluded that justice is a human creation. I think he was completely right. We make awkward attempts to create a sense of justice. Obviously it doesn't work very well, but at least we make the attempts and hold on to the ideal.

There is no explanation as to why my brother was attacked and reduced to this condition in the latter part of his life. There was no reason for it.

I'd been so sad not to be with my mother when she died. I was sad I wasn't able to see Driss before he died. I was so sad I couldn't visit my brother in hospital more often. I visited him only once in Strasbourg because I was detained in Nacton; then later, several times when he was in Toulouse. But yet again, I was so sad that I couldn't see him one last time before he died.

That year was a difficult time, full of sorrow. I needed to weep. Weeping makes you surrender, give up.

I settled down in Under Shollond. I liked the house. It was different from Shollond Hill, although it also had beautiful architecture. But it wasn't as comfortable. It was further down the hill, and it was damp, without a decent heating system. I bought gas stoves and electric stoves but nothing helped. In winter especially it was really cold and dank. I got frequent colds and sore throats, but I was determined to stay there. As much as I am in love with Douglas and with Seeing, I am in love with England. I don't know why, but I feel good in England. There is an ambience of serenity and kindness and respect for each other.

The following January I had a stroke. I was at home. I didn't feel well and I had a pain in my arm. Dominique called me, as she often did. I said I wasn't feeling well and thought my rheumatism might be flaring up. I described the pain to her and she said, 'Oh no, you are having a heart attack. You must call the hospital right now!' I did so and they immediately took me in and treated me.

I realised, of course, that I couldn't count on Dominique for help, as she was 2,000 or 3,000 kilometres away. My children said, 'This is ridiculous. You are on your own in Nacton. Your best friends live all over England, they can't come to help you. And we've hardly seen you in twenty years.'

So I felt I had to go back to France.

I put the house on the market but, because of the financial crisis, it took three years to sell. Richard Lang tried to buy it. He is like Douglas' spiritual son, so that would have been wonderful; the house could have been a second Shollond Hill. But it didn't work out. Eventually my children and my friends helped me move back to France.

It is true that the place where you have been happy, where you have loved and been loved, itself captures something of that love. I went back to Nacton a few times, and every time my heart immediately felt full of joy and happiness.

I'm pleased that the people who finally bought Under Shollond really love it. They haven't changed it much, and what they have changed is what I would have changed myself, had I had the money. They turned the attic into a habitable loft and the garage into an extra room. They built a wooden hut in the garden to use as an office. Ann Jackson, who still lives in Nacton, sometimes meets them. They keep telling her that when Catherine visits again she must come and see the house.

Ann also looks after Douglas' grave. She cleans the headstone and does the weeding. When I die I want to be buried next to Douglas. My name is already on the gravestone. I asked the engravers to engrave my date of birth there, so that they would only have to add the date of my death. But they refused to do it because they thought it was a bad omen. So they will need to lift out the stone to engrave the rest when I am gone. My children want to keep half of my ashes in France; the other half I want to be put in a box next to Douglas.

'The other day you mentioned the difference between your love for Douglas and your love for Driss?'

My love for Driss and my love for Douglas are two different worlds, absolutely. They are at different levels of consciousness. In fact, my whole life has been a slow journey, slowly moving towards Douglas, from unconscious seeing to conscious Seeing.

My first love, my love for Driss, was a conditional love. He had a likeness to my father and reminded me of him in many ways. When we first met he talked a lot about physics; he was still studying chemistry at that time to please his own father. He was handsome, charming and brilliant, and we were the same age. He was full of life and a passion for beauty: we both loved literature, music, art and nature. All this was attractive, and that is why I fell in love with him. It was a passionate love. Probably it was the same for him. Later, my love for him became less conditional because I came to love him at a deeper level.

I had always thought that my love would help Driss solve his problems, but I have since learned that love does not solve anybody's psychological problems; it just won't. I know that his problems stemmed from the fact that he had been uprooted from his family and had experienced humiliation; he was conditioned by a very particular familial context. Moreover, it was difficult for him to adjust to France and to Europe. I also came to realise that, like so many artists, he had no sense of responsibility. His obsession above all was to write: that was even more important to him than his love for me and his children.

My love for Douglas was immediately an unconditional love. You can say that I fell for him because he was a father figure, but I never saw him as that. I saw him as a lover, and at that level our relationship was perfect too. My love was unconditional, without limit. I knew he was all and everything for me and always would be, whatever happened. He used to say, 'I would go and share Seeing in hell' – and I would have followed him there.

'And not only for the heat!' she adds, with a laugh.

Seeing makes it possible for me to adapt
to everything everywhere.

8
The art of disappearing

Catherine asks if I would mind driving her car to help her with some shopping; she can't drive herself anymore. When we leave her apartment she meets her neighbour who is 90 years old. The two women talk and laugh for a while in French. When we get into the elevator she tells me that her neighbour warned her not to forget to wear her earrings when she goes out: 'You might catch a cold!' 'French humour,' she laughs.

The car and the traffic are not very different from the way they are in Holland, and I manage to drive us to a big supermarket. A few hours later we are back, with many bags full of food which disappears into the freezer and the cupboards, her supply for the coming weeks.

We have a piece of French brioche and a cup of tea. She adds a lot of sugar. 'I don't see why it is bad for you,' she says. 'I like sugar.'

When I left England at first I wanted to go to Paris; I have many Seeing friends there. One is José le Roy, a professor of philosophy who is a dear friend and dedicated to Seeing. He gives workshops in his apartment every month and has written several books about Seeing and philosophy. He's often invited to give workshops or lectures all over France. Two of my sons also live in Paris; I stayed with them for a while. Then I saw the price of apartments: Paris is incredibly expensive, just like London. I can't afford it. So I decided that the sensible thing to do would be to go to the south of France, to Montpellier, where my other children live.

At first, in Montpellier, I was so sad that I couldn't think much. I rented a furnished studio that looked out over the sea in Palavas-les-Flots, which is about fifteen minutes away from Montpellier by car. I thought that the sea would help me, and it did, it made me peaceful. I was as happy as I could be there. I walked along the beach every day. Sea gulls and a few friends came to visit me regularly. My children too. And I drove into Montpellier whenever I wanted to.

Then I realised I couldn't stay there; the rent was too high and I was getting fed up with Palavas. It's full of old couples and ladies with permed hair and dogs who walk along the beach. It's not a very inspiring environment. Moreover, my apartment was in the tourist part of town, which gets very crowded in the summer. I realised also that I didn't have enough money to buy a house in Montpellier, because the South of France is expensive too.

Then I remembered our house in the mountains, in Graissessac. Douglas came there with me several times. I thought I would feel that he was with me, and I would be able to have wonderful walks up there. The house is in a beautiful location, looking down over a sea of mountains.

Graissessac is a mining village, and poor miners used to live in the house, which was actually no more than walls and a roof.

There was only one tap, the wiring was in a dangerous state, and the roof and floors were full of holes. In the summer we used to camp there; it was like an upmarket camping ground. I had bought it extremely cheaply back in 1980 with my son Michel, for the equivalent of about fifteen thousand euros. There are actually two houses adjoining, and my daughter Laurence owns the other one. I thought the house had great potential so I invested the money from Under Shollond in it to make it habitable.

I had the roof repaired and insulated in accordance with current regulations. I replaced the rotten window frames and had double glazing put in. I had the house totally rewired and replumbed. There wasn't a bathroom, so we installed one. The floors were reconcreted and retiled. I bought some new pieces of furniture to supplement the furniture I'd brought over from Nacton. And that was it.

My only mistake was not to realise that I was going to get old and subject to the handicaps of age.

When I came back to France I was 78 years old and still fit. After my eightieth birthday, however, things began to deteriorate. I had trouble with one of my hips, my heart and other minor issues: nothing very serious, but living in Graissessac became a problem.

The house is built on a slope and the only access to it is via a steep flight of steps. My hip used to hurt so much when I climbed up or down them that it became impossible for me to live there anymore. It also became difficult for me to go on walks, because the starting point of any walk from my house meant going uphill.

Also, although the village has a medical centre, a pharmacy, a very small shop for vegetables and groceries and a pizzeria, as well as a little market on Thursdays, there is no bakery there anymore, no butcher's ... So driving was essential.

The life that little Catherine had planned in her head

(when the head had not disappeared) went as follows: 'I'm going to translate more of Douglas' works and I'm going to give workshops everywhere.' In fact, only the translating is happening. Everything Richard asks me to translate I do with incomparable joy, because then I am with Douglas the whole time.

The workshops haven't worked out, so far. I did give two workshops in Montpellier, but they weren't great. Montpellier is a difficult place – Cartesian, one might say: the people tend to overvalue logic and the intellect. There are also lots of other things on offer here, notably in terms of the entertainment business.

To make matters worse, on top of my existing health problems, I had a car accident, which meant that I just couldn't do the workshop I'd planned last October. Ever since, I've said, 'Next month I'll give a workshop' – but I just haven't been able to yet.

It's so strange that I've ended up in Montpellier. I didn't particularly want to. But I'm beginning to realise that I may be here for a reason. Maybe my job now is not to give workshops but to help my children. For twenty years I left them in favour of Douglas; I came to France only once or twice a year during that time. Maybe I have to make up for that now. And it seems to be better for my children and grandchildren that I'm back here. Everybody tells me so. Nevertheless, I'm still thinking of giving workshops again!

My children are not particularly interested in Seeing. Stephan is a great poet. He knows all about Seeing but he doesn't really practise it. He is also a businessman and a musician. His job is very demanding, and he has a band and has to organise all the concerts and the recordings. Life's moving too fast for him.

I think speed is very bad. When you are caught up in a fast-paced life, it's very difficult to practise Seeing.

Having said which, at one of our workshops in Nacton there was a woman who just didn't get Seeing. Stephan happened to be there, and he showed it to her very clearly. Afterwards she said to me, 'Thanks to your son, I got it.' It often happens like that. One day we had a guy at a workshop in France and he didn't get it. He went back home and his wife asked him, 'How was it?' He told her all about the experiments and she got it immediately. And then she showed him and this time he got it! Funny, isn't it?

As for my children, they don't really want to be interested in Seeing because it's their mother's thing. Of course, if I try to show them, it's going to sound to them as if their mother is telling them what to do. I used to try, but I don't anymore. I am sure my children will come to it later. Right now they're working out their conditioning from their father: they have to prove that what they're doing is the right thing for them to be doing, and that they are doing it well.

I would like so very much to be able to share with them this state you get when you see who you are, when you see you are no thing and every thing. When you are empty consciousness, wide open to the world, and there is only peace and joy and love springing from the bottom of Being. I'd like so much for them to see that we all come from the same empty, clear, conscious, infinite space. Many people understand it intellectually from the experiments because it is obvious: it's reasonable, it's sensible, it's a fact. But seeing the evidence for it and living from it are totally different matters.

Every one of us is looking out of the same clear, aware, impersonal space. When we see that we all are this universal consciousness there are no barriers between us. And when you really live this, it has effects on the people you meet.

You go to a supermarket and you come to the till. In France, unlike in England, shop assistants are not always very pleasant, and perhaps the person on the till is someone who is fed up with her job. But when you look at her with a wide open heart, seeing her from who you are, seeing that she's looking at you from the same wide open awareness as you, she immediately lightens up. I've noticed it again and again. She starts to smile, and for a few minutes a special relationship develops, and everything is different.

To live from who one really is changes life. I can live with physical pain and my handicaps with greater serenity and patience, because if I turn my attention around to the Centre and let myself sink to the bottom of Being, where there is no Catherine anymore, I find peace, and the pain remains at a distance.

I feel lucky in every way. Everything has come into place. My son Stephan has provided me with this apartment in Montpellier because I couldn't stay on my own in Graissessac anymore, and this apartment has turned out to be a paradise. It could have been a dark flat in an old building in a narrow street, because Montpellier has many apartments like that. But it's wide open to the sky and the legendary southern sunshine, there is a large terrace where I've put lots of flowers (my best friends), and it's very comfortable. What more is needed? I am lucky with all my good friends who come to visit me. I am lucky with my children who take care of me so lovingly.

Our French friends used to call Douglas their master and me the eternal mother. It's strange, but sometimes I really feel as though I am everyone's mother.

Attention is most important. I remember Alan Rowlands directing an interesting experiment in Nacton. He put an object in the middle of the room and asked us to look at it. And everybody found out that just concentrating their attention on this object changed what they saw. The object was enlightened by our attention, and it was easy to see its beauty.

Looking at the beauty that is everywhere is another way for me to remain at peace. The media only shows the bad things that are happening in the world, but there are many good things. When I look at nature it is absolutely beautiful. I am enchanted by the flowers here. And there is music; I often listen to music. And there are paintings. Montpellier has a museum with wonderful exhibitions. There are wonderful books and poetry. All this enables me to live in a beautiful world. The world is not only conflicts and killing: a beautiful, enchanting world exists too. Both worlds exist, but we tend to forget the beautiful enchanting one.

I always remember Douglas saying one day: 'The world might be awful – the universe might be awful – but it's still worth existing because it produced Mozart.'

It is true: Mozart and all the others. Human beings are continually producing beautiful things. The beautiful things that are being created right now may not yet be well-known, but I am sure they are there. There are some wonderful modern artists. I don't know much about modern music: I haven't found anything I really like, but one has to get accustomed to things.

Seeing gives me that too: the ability to adjust to any conditions and not to be attached to anything.

I have moved around the world so often. That was my destiny as a little one: I was thrown out of my earthly home when I was seven and a half. I have never found an earthly home since, except in Nacton. And with Douglas, I found the way to our real home, the home I knew when I was a child, my

Real Home that in fact I had never left.

Now, wherever I am, my home is at my Centre.

Only now have I come to the knowledge
that I know nothing.

9

Life is my guru

The phone rings again. Catherine looks at caller display and says she has to take the call. I sit out on the balcony.

Not for a moment this past week have I had the feeling that either one of us was superior in wisdom or practice to the other. On the contrary, our differences have become more and more insignificant. Still, she has lived Seeing a few decades longer than I have, which makes me curious about her vision at this point in her life.

When she finishes her call she tells me that lately she likes to say 'à toujours' instead of goodbye. À toujours ... Till always ...

I ask, 'Now that you are in your eighties – what is your conclusion about life and Seeing?'

Well, a lot has happened to me in my life. You can just live life without trying to understand what is happening to you.

But if you live your life thoroughly and sincerely, with love and attention even when something is painful, then you can come to see why the pain is happening to you. You can learn from it, although you sometimes have to wait a while before you see the reason for it.

I never had a guru. I had a spiritual friend, the great Tibetan lama, Kalu Rinpoche. And after him I had Douglas. But neither of them was really a guru. Kalu Rinpoche didn't want to be a guru; he was just a great friend. And Douglas was not my guru; he didn't want to be a guru for anyone.

'Don't believe what I say: test it for yourself,' he kept saying. 'You are the sole authority of yourself.'

He was the man I loved, and a man I admired for his genius in finding effective ways to reach our true nature.

In fact, I never wanted a guru because you would have to believe what he or she said; you would have to worship them, which I would hate to do. My guru was life itself.

I lived through the war, which was a terrible time. This showed me from an early age that you should keep a distance from material things and not be attached to them, because they can quickly disappear. The only really important thing is life itself. After that I made some wrong choices with my relationships and friends, and I learned that you really must pay attention when you are becoming close to someone.

I came from a narrow-minded culture. My family was bourgeois in an intellectual sense: not rich but well-educated. They were lovely people, but they were afraid of the Japanese – whom they called the yellow peril – and of the Bolsheviks. My grandmother used to say, 'I peel the vegetables for the whole family so that, when the Bolsheviks get here, they will see that I have the hands of a working woman and not of a rich woman, and they won't behead me.' They were afraid of anything that was different.

This too was a great lesson for me. I felt repressed in that family. Not because of my father, though: he had already died by the time I was ten years old. And my mother was a lovely person, just a bowl of tenderness like women should be. But there was a narrow-mindedness based in ignorance that I wanted to get away from.

It's not so strange that I should fall in love with this young man from Morocco who was an artist with no money at all. My Moroccan husband opened my mind up both to the Arab world and to the world as a whole. I became interested in other cultures and was no longer limited to white European people and their cultures.

Having to live with very, very little money was also a guru for me. I was able to do it because we had so much love (which also was a lesson for me). I only missed money when I was left on my own and couldn't buy clothes for my children, which was embarrassing. Otherwise I always managed to juggle my finances. Sometimes I had to borrow from moneylenders and pay back at high interest rates. Nowadays, when you have five children, you get a lot of money from the government, but in my day you didn't.

And then, when I had big problems and was really suffering, I met my spiritual friend Kalu Rinpoche, who was to me the incarnation of the Clear Light, and I learned to put a distance between outside events and myself.

The experience I'd had when I was sixteen years old of this loving Light was a guru. From then on I knew that this Light is life, real life. That's why it made sense to me when Kalu Rinpoche talked to me about the Clear Light: I had already seen it. The only thing left to know was how to get back to this Light at will. When I met Douglas, he gave me the answer.

Life is still my guru, I am still learning. I have to learn to live without Douglas. I am much better about it now but I've had to learn to live with only his presence within me. The

Light, which he showed me how to reach, is helping me all the time.

All that I have endured has taught me to understand what other people are enduring. I have learned to see that whatever happens in the world, human stories repeat themselves time and again.

And also that things pass. I used to attach myself to people and places with all my heart. This life, however, has shown me that nothing lasts. It has forced me to accept things, and to accept them willingly. It has taught me to see that we are not in control of anything. When you're young, you think, 'I'm going to do this and that.' And then you come to realise that you are not in control. Then you see that things just happen, and our only choice is to willingly accept them.

Only now in my life have I come to the knowledge that I know nothing. I am discovering everything anew. I realise there are so many different points of view, so many different answers to the same question, that I think the only answer is to be here, here in the Land of Clarity. As soon as you go into the world of things, it's so complicated that nothing is really certain or clear. I used to have very strong convictions and beliefs about this or that, but I have noticed that for me they are not true anymore. Everything changes all the time, including your convictions.

At one point in my life I thought that the only solution was to live in the Christian way, to be very charitable and open. This is true on one level but it is not true on others. And it is not true in the absolute: the absolute, in fact, means to disappear. That's why I say that for me the art of life is the art of disappearing.

Before meeting Douglas I thought that after I had retired

I would go and help in third world countries because the people there needed help. Then I realised that sometimes this isn't the right thing to do. Sometimes you shouldn't help people, because you are preventing them from learning – like parents who always want to protect their children and thereby prevent them from growing. Difficulties and suffering help you to mature.

Imagine a country by the sea where the people are poor and starving. One day there comes a man who knows how to fish. He starts to fish and soon catches a great haul. The natives are full of admiration. 'How do you manage that?' they say. 'Please give us some too!' 'Sure I will give you fish.' He is so good at fishing that he gives them for free. But this isn't a good solution: now they depend on him.

Of course, if you want to think in terms of politics or economics, you would say: the man who knows how to fish should make the others pay for the fish. He doesn't want to teach them: he wants to keep his power over them by selling them what they need. Economically that makes sense. But not ethically. Helping people by giving them fish for free is no good either. The better answer is to teach them how to fish for themselves.

What I do believe is that, so long as we are incarnated, we should share. I think this is true at all levels. First, we have to learn to share objects. Young children have a tendency to not want to share. I remember putting great emphasis on showing my children they had to share, that they were happier when they shared. I think it's possible to teach this to young children. And if everyone accepted this, the result would be obvious: the world wouldn't be in such a terrible state, would it? It's really unbelievable that people can't see that.

Emotions and ideas should also be shared. It is very bad luck if you've been conditioned to be unable to show or share your emotions. It's also important to be able to share your ideas and your discoveries, like Douglas did. To me it seems that something that is never shared doesn't really exist: it only comes into existence when it's given out.

That is why I said in a workshop recently that I think it is so important to share Seeing, because the world needs it. One aspect of Seeing is that it shows us our oneness with the world, with other creatures and, of course, especially with other human beings. Once you have seen this oneness and you really live it, you can't willingly hurt anyone else.

❁

Some people say that once you see who you are nothing will affect you anymore and there is no need for you to interfere with whatever might be happening. I don't agree with that. The Buddhists say that void is form and form is void, and this is so evident in Douglas' Card experiment[6]. You can't separate the clarity here from the objects out there. The objects, the forms and the movement are in the clarity, they belong to it; they are one. So the dramas we live through in our human history also belong to the void or clarity. They are part of it.

I think that the only thing my spiritual life has really given me is the ability to change the way I look at things. Looking from who I really am is a different point of view. I am not influenced by what is happening, although I am part of it.

Take, for example, the problems of my children and grandchildren. When I talk to them at the level of the drama, I get really involved. But as soon as I stop identifying with that level and fall back into my viewpoint as a Seer, that puts

6. See Appendix.

everything in place. But the dramas are still part of me. The drama of the story of the little one, is one with the One. It is within the One; there is no separation. I think this is very important.

I have been affected by what goes on in the world all my life. I feel I am the world. There is so much suffering in the world right now, and for me one way to remain at peace with that is to send love. When I see who I am, I can send love through the world to all these people. I don't know if it works but I believe that it does. A little drop of love.

Pierre Rabhi, a French writer and environmentalist, tells the story of the *colibri*, a little hummingbird who lived in a big forest. One day a huge fire breaks out in the forest and all the animals run out, screaming and crying. As they watch the flames consuming the trees and destroying the whole forest, they feel overwhelmed and powerless, and say to each other that there's nothing they can do.

Except for the little hummingbird: this tiny bird quietly flies up and down to the nearest stream and back to the fire, and each time it drops one drop of water on the big fire. All the other animals watch and laugh at the bird: 'How stupid you are, silly little bird! How do you think you are going to put out this terrible fire with your little drop of water?'

And the little hummingbird replies, 'I'm playing my part in the best way I can.'

That is what I feel I have been trying to do with my life, without realising it, having seen so many horrors, so much distress and pain since the age of seven. I decided that I should do what I could in the world around me.

My first drop of water was to try and help Garry Davis, who said that frontiers are man-made. After that there was my love story with Driss, a penniless Arab artist. Of course, I was just in love, but I also realised from this that love does not stop at frontiers. Then I worked for a French radio station, France Culture, for which Driss and I adapted many African stories against racism.

When I was a teacher at the Lycée, I tried to share with my pupils the feeling that we are all brothers. Of the shows we put on, the most successful was a play about peace adapted from Bernard Benson's book, *Le Livre de la Paix* (*The Book of Peace*). I also worked for an association called Education and The Third World, whose purpose was to help developing schools in the poorest countries and raise funds to train teachers there.

And eventually I dedicated my life to Douglas and to Seeing, which I hope is going to be an enormous help in putting out the big fire that is devastating the world: the fire of selfishness and separation.

Seeing is simply a way to help people love each other. Jesus Christ said we have to love each other, which is very difficult so long as one identifies only with the little one. But when you see clearly that what you really, really are is this immensity, this clear limitless awareness, and that we are all One, then loving one another is much easier.

So my role in life is to send love around me to all my friends, to the people in this building, to my children and to anyone else I encounter. Love is the only thing that counts: that is my conclusion at the end of my life. I have always thought so, but now I try to live it. I really see that this is the only thing that has results on the people I meet and live with. The best thing I can do is to care for other people, and to constantly see that I am them.

From the perspective of the 84 years that I've lived through, I think that a great mistake has been made about women's liberation. Women are not liberated: their social situation is a little better, that's all. On the one hand they get more consideration and can take a job; but on the other hand all they've been trying to do is to imitate men. They act like masculine women. It makes me feel sad to see, for example, female executives trying to be men. They wanted to be free and all they could do was to imitate their dominators.

Look at Margaret Thatcher in England and the awful way she behaved. She helped turn the western world into a world dominated by money; a world that revolves around things and money – not human beings anymore. One can see she was a free woman but she acted like a man, heartless and without sensitivity. She put her job and power before everything else. I believe that that's not how women are made. We are not made to try and imitate men.

In the first place, we have the power to give life, which is a great power and not only connected with giving birth. Spiritually and physically speaking, it is also about giving life to the people around us. We were originally created to show tenderness, such as the tenderness shown in nurturing our babies. The world is dying for lack of tenderness. It seems to me that what we need to bring back to the world is this approach of tenderness and creativity. Deep in their hearts most women feel loving and tender, but life often toughens them up.

I think we have missed an opportunity here, although maybe it's not too late; maybe we can still change something in society by means of feminine qualities. If the world is going to change, I'm sure it will be through women.

In the west we are very lucky and privileged as far as women's rights are concerned. Our rights were recognised about fifty years ago. In France it was thanks to General de

Gaulle that we got the right to vote. The generations that have followed since have been born with this right. But in many countries women are still repressed. A possible explanation for this repression is that men are afraid of our creativity and our power of giving life.

But before we bring tenderness and creativity into the world, we must first fight for all women everywhere to have the same rights as we do. I feel very concerned about and involved with all women everywhere. When I was in India I met many women who were fighting for their rights. Sometimes they did it secretly and in minor ways; sometimes they devoted their whole lives to protest about and expose the injustices that they had suffered. Sometimes they lost their lives in this cause.

Secondly, what I like to say about so-called women's liberation is that women are not free to be themselves at all. In order to be accepted and to be successful, they have to follow the dictates of fashion. You must have breasts like this, you must weigh that much, have lips this way and a nose that way. The rules about appearance are very strict and most women try to conform to them, which is very bad for their true nature.

Women have become sex objects. You can't see even an advertisement for milk or sweets or anything else without a pair of breasts or buttocks or a naked woman along with it. That seems to be the rule. To me it is unbelievable that the female body is always and everywhere offered up for consumption.

A sexual relationship is beautiful when it happens with love. From what I see on television and the internet, sex is quickly turning into pornography. It's way too much. It's like butchery: all the body parts are exposed, the penis, the vagina, all of it. To me this seems dehumanising, both for women and for men.

There are so-called spiritual people who say that the world is an illusion, and I just don't understand this. I don't agree. One can't say that everything is illusion. I think it's an insult to people who are really suffering, who are repressed and put in jail and tortured. To say that it's just illusion shows total insensitivity. I feel for all the people in the world who are suffering: they are me and I am them.

I think there are two realities: one is the earthly reality for the incarnated little ones; the other is the big One, the absolute reality. And the reality of the little ones is contained within the absolute reality. When you reach your Centre, when you reach the Clear Light, the two realities become one. The Clear Light is within everything and within every one of us. Here the two meet.

The stories of the little ones are real but they pass, of course; that is why people say it's an illusion. But although something passes, it's still real, it's still something people have to endure.

Form is void and void is form. The void is full with form. Obviously there are two realities: the reality of the void and the reality of the forms. But they are one. Two within One. They are not separated: the reality of human stories is contained within the absolute reality.

I know there are people like, for example, the extraordinary Dutch woman who wrote letters from a concentration camp. I have the book here: *Letters from Westerbork* by Etty Hillesum. She managed to see the Clear Light even in the midst of the horrors she was going through. But these kinds of people are very, very rare. I don't know if I would have been able to be like her in that situation. And Etty Hillesum didn't say that suffering is an illusion.

I am living both realities at the same time – aren't you? I

am living the joy of being here with these beautiful flowers and with you next to me in this lovely apartment. And at the same time I know it is a very limited reality, and I'm looking at it from the Clear Light, which is happening now within everything.

Seeing gives us the great privilege of being able to be in the big One, to use Douglas' terminology. Or if I put it in other words: in the Clear Light, in the absolute reality. And at the same time we are aware of what is going on and are enjoying or suffering it.

I can also put it the other way around: living the present moment and enjoying it, and at the same time Seeing that this is all happening within my real nature, within who I really am.

These flowers are not an illusion. I like them so much and I can see how they flourish, that they are beautiful and respond to my love. However, all this will pass, whereas who I am won't: that is the difference.

For me the most important thing has become to live from this, rather than only talking about it.

10
The evolution of consciousness

It's our last day. We sit for the last time at the kitchen table where she has shared her memories, her life and her vision. Paradoxically I realise how little I know about her. And yet I know her; here, in the Silence, we are the same. This is almost palpable in her presence.

I look at my list of notes and questions and decide to put it away. There's nothing to complete. We sit and wait and see what comes up.

More and more I realise that I am not Catherine at all, the little Catherine. I am the eternal universal consciousness, experiencing life in the form of Catherine, just as you are the universal consciousness experiencing being you. At the root of ourselves, at the core of ourselves, we are this universal clear consciousness. That is why we are One. If we take the trouble to turn our attention around and reach this wonderful place, the universal consciousness within ourselves, we shall see it. I think this is very important.

Little Catherine is only a vehicle, a tool. But I don't become the tool. If I pick up a hammer, it's an extension of my body, but I don't become the hammer. If Catherine is my instrument I don't totally become Catherine, I use Catherine. That is why you have to look after your instrument: you have to keep it in good shape if you want to be able to use it. That's why I'm trying to keep going as best as I can, because obviously I haven't died yet. That's why I'm trying to improve my physical condition, so that my instrument works a little better again.

I am learning and learning – nothing but learning. Learning how to be more here. Learning to see what I really am more often. And learning how to be slow. Everything is really slow now, which makes you look at things differently. It puts a distance between yourself and the things you used to think were important. When you take the time to just be and look from here at everything, you see that all of that is not so urgent. You don't have to do this or that. Whereas when you identify yourself with your little person you think, 'Oh, I must do this, I must do that' – which is often not really necessary at all.

For me the most important thing has become to live from this, rather than simply talking about it. This is obviously what is asked of me now. In order to be with the problems of my family I have to live from here, otherwise I can't do it. Being slow helps me tremendously.

I am also learning to give up attachment to my appearance. This body is deteriorating all the time. When I look at my body I think, 'This is incredible – this isn't me!' Only now am I getting the message that this body really is a temporary envelope that I was given to manage during this short lifetime.

It is not who I am. It is just a tool. And that is good because I don't care much about my appearance anymore. I do care about it for the sake of others. I don't want to have my children face the spectacle of a deteriorating old lady. Your children especially become sad when they see someone they love getting into a bad state.

I am also learning to be patient. Douglas always used to tell me, 'Catherine, you are so impatient.' He was right: I am an impatient lady. Little Catherine is very impatient. Only now am I learning patience. I have to, because everything that happens to me, physically speaking, takes so long to heal. At least I hope it will heal; I'm not sure that it will.

The art of life is really the art of disappearing. I am constantly learning the art of disappearing. Peace and joy and serenity belong to the place where, as little ones, we are gone. I am not here as Catherine. As Catherine I must disappear in order to be the big One, to be pure unconditional love, serenity and timelessness. All this I become when I disappear as the little one. It's not always easy.

So when I talk about the art of disappearing, that's actually what I practise. Every time I find myself caught in the prison of little Catherine, I know she has to go. Then I have to practise the essence of Seeing: turn my attention around 180 degrees, look in and see that there is no Catherine here above my shoulders. Here is nothing at all, absolutely nothing.

The world exists, and I can let the flow of love move into it. Actually I don't like the word 'love' anymore because it is so misused and overused. It's more like compassion, but not compassion in the sense of feeling superior to the people you have compassion for. Actually, I don't like the word 'compassion' either. What I mean is a feeling of oneness with the whole world, with my flowers here, with you, with this bird, with any creature.

You can only have this sense of oneness if you disappear as a little one. Then it is bliss, then you are free. Free to be, free to love and free to accept everything. As long as you are in the prison of the little one, you are conditioned. It's very painful then to accept the hard things. But when you disappear, you see that there is no little one here; there is no Catherine here above my shoulders. All there is is infinite clear consciousness. Then I am free, and everything is different.

This winter I went through a lot of physical suffering. I discovered that physical pain can be so strong that you just sink into it. Then you are drowned in it, and there is nothing left of you except a block of pain. You have lost every connection with your little person, and with spirit and Seeing. There is nothing left of you, so it's impossible to connect with that. It is truly what St John of the Cross called the dark night of the soul; it is atrocious.

When the pain gets a little less, Seeing can help you. If you are used to turning your attention around, you can do it immediately then. When the pain became a little bit less, thanks to Douglas' experiments I was able to find the Light fairly quickly again.

Before this experience I had thought I had disappeared as the little Catherine, but then I realised that I hadn't really disappeared at all. In this experience of severe physical suffering, however, the little one disappeared completely. It is total humiliation for the little one, because you become just a bag of flesh being looked after by other people. You can't wash yourself, you can't do anything, it's terrible. You are just an object in the hands of other people. That is real, real disappearing.

Suffering without Seeing is terrible but suffering with Seeing is bearable. When I came out of this abyss of pain I rediscovered the Clear Light again. And not even slowly, because Seeing is always instantaneous!

Afterwards I felt grateful because for the first time I really felt in my bones, rather than simply understood, that this body is a mere vehicle that is lent to us for a lifetime. It is precious because it's our instrument and we have to look after it. But it really has nothing to do with who we really are. The body changes day by day; every day it gets older and every day it gets a little more damaged. In the end you don't recognise it anymore. The beauty I had when I was young was a joke because it was there for such a short time. Now there is nothing left of it.

The only thing left that absolutely never changes is who I really am. That has nothing to do with this mortal body, because it is always well. I am 84: this body is like an old vehicle with broken and replaced parts, and soon it will be sent to the car cemetery. But not who I really am. What is looking at the world within me is exactly the same as what was looking at the world when I was five years old. I remember looking at the Vosges Mountains, and it was the same aware space looking at the world.

To me it is a tremendous experience to really perceive this. It is also freeing, because I'm really not identifying with this body anymore. When I look at myself in the mirror now, I think, 'I have nothing to do with that person over there.' Here it is completely open.

What I'd like to say concerning our global evolution is that I think that Darwin was right. Physically speaking, we have evolved from tiny bacteria into human beings; that is evolution.

And although the human being seems to be the pinnacle of evolution, it seems to me that this is not the end point. What could come after a human being?

What is left for us – and for nature also – is the evolution of consciousness. I think there are many levels of consciousness, and slowly, slowly mankind will attain to higher levels. Probably there will always exist low levels and high levels simultaneously, but it seems now that there are increasingly higher levels of consciousness among us human beings. Maybe the last step of evolution is the evolution through levels of consciousness. Of course, consciousness itself can't change or evolve, but our level of consciousness can.

I've recently noticed that a whole wave of people is getting interested in full consciousness, *la pleine conscience*. To me this is indicative of a higher level of consciousness, even though it's not the end of the process. People like Douglas are helping us to take a great step forward.

I don't think that this will change the world into a perfect place but it might make it a little better. I know some people say that nothing has changed but I don't think that's true. A few things have changed, even for women. Women are still oppressed in many parts of the world but less so than centuries ago. Nowadays there are more countries where women are fighting for and winning their rights. Also, there is a greater sense of solidarity all over the planet.

In other areas, of course, we are now faced with the terrible problem of the barbaric cruelty of militant Islam. Maybe you can't expect to have a steady evolution. Maybe it goes step by step: a step forwards and a step backwards.

But if one could spread Seeing, if people could see that it is a fact that we are all the same and that we all come from the same Clear Light, then maybe that would create a better understanding among people. Most of the bad and terrible things that are happening for humanity happen because people think that they are different. They think that they are separate. If they could see that the differences are so superficial and that on a profound level we are the same, maybe it would be easier for them to accept others, if not to love them. I just think that it's a possibility.

There's a story I've heard about the hundred monkeys. On an island there lived a big family of monkeys and they ate potatoes. They stole the potatoes from the fields and ate them without washing them. One day, one monkey – probably a female monkey! – had the idea of washing the potato, and she found that this made it so much nicer to eat. She showed her family and her friends, and all the monkey mothers around started to wash their potatoes. When the hundredth monkey did it, then, all of a sudden, the monkeys on other islands started to wash their potatoes too.

A small percentage of people think or do something for a certain length of time, and then all of a sudden the whole species is doing it. I don't know if this is true but it's what I believe: that the more individuals there are among us who are trying to See and find out who they really are, the more Seeing will spread. What Richard Lang is doing in sharing Seeing throughout the world is extraordinary. And we are all doing what we can.

The point, though, is that you can't know what people will do with it; it's out of our hands. We can spread the news but we can't force people into practising it or into really living it. It is a personal choice or decision to live from this vision, or not. For some, it may never come to life and will remain a nice intellectual view.

Living from it, however, is much more difficult because that changes everything. Yet the key to our global evolution lies in the number of people who are really doing something with it. This is everyone's responsibility.

Sometimes I got so excited because Douglas and I were

holding huge workshops and people were absolutely in love with Douglas, but then nothing seemed to happen. I don't think they changed their lives at all. There was no feedback. Sometimes that was a little disappointing, although you never know. On the other hand, we've had people who have said, 'I met Douglas fifteen years ago in America. At the time I thought that it sounded all very good but then I forgot about it. Now I'm back, and I know you are right: this is the answer to everything.' It happens that people who have been involved in Seeing and have left, sometimes even to follow other gurus or do something else, suddenly come back.

In France, José le Roy is passing on Seeing. José is dedicated, clear and faithful to Douglas' way. He doesn't modify anything. Because it has happened that people have manipulated Douglas' experiments for their own reasons. Douglas told me that this would happen, and that you couldn't do anything about it. People might use them for purposes of personal development or to enhance their self-confidence, to become a 'know it all' person.

You can turn any kind of spiritual teaching into an ego booster. It's the same with yoga. Some of the people I studied and practised with at the Yoga Institute in India have become famous yoga teachers in France. Now they're saying, 'I am someone who can do the most extraordinary postures' – which isn't what it's about at all.

Sometimes I feel as though I'm a thousand years old. I've had a fascinating and happy life, and it's all gone so quickly. I tell young people to enjoy every moment, because suddenly, there's the end. I realise how incredibly short life is. Everything is now. All the memories are now. My life has gone by in a flash. It is just a point now; all the rest has sunk in time. My message to everyone is to enjoy the present moment and the beauty of it wherever you see it – and it is everywhere – and to marvel at the miracle of life, of being alive and of existing.

We sit back and are silent for a while. Then I remember what I forgot to ask: 'How do you feel about dying?'

I am ready to go. Dying tomorrow is fine by me. But if I am still here, it's because I am needed; maybe for my children or maybe for some other reason that I don't yet know about.

I am not afraid of death at all right now, because I feel it's going to be like seeing who I am for ever, being who I am for ever. I see dying like walking into the sea: walking along the beach and going in. I don't know because, after all, no one has ever exactly come back to tell us. Even with near death experiences, the doctors say that if we have these experiences it's because we haven't really gone into death; there are still some perceptions left.

So I don't know: it's the only mystery that still remains.

The only thing I'm sure of is that I'm not this little person called Catherine. I can see that this body is a vehicle that was given to me at my birth, which moves along through this existence. It's now obvious I can't identify with it since there is nothing left from the original form. Many of the parts have deteriorated so much that they've had to be replaced. Whereas what is driving it has not changed a bit. The vehicle is now ready for the scrap heap, but what I really am is absolutely intact.

Actually there are still two mysteries for me. The first is: how did this life occur, or how did consciousness appear? And the second is: what's left after we die? Does anything of the identity survive? For example, in the case of Douglas: is there something of his identity left somewhere that is still intact? Or has he totally dissolved, merged in the universal consciousness, for a new reincarnation or whatever? I just don't know.

Some people are absolutely convinced that there is something left of our individual identity. Some friends, trying to be nice, say to me, 'Don't worry! Douglas is looking after you wherever he is.' But I'm not sure that's true. I know Douglas is here in my heart; he lives through me now. But is there a possibility that somewhere in this eternal limitless space he could really engage with my life? It could just be wishful thinking.

For a moment we speculate about the possibilities.

When we go into death, we will discover the answers. I think it's going to be fascinating. The only thing we can do for now is to try to ensure the stability of our Seeing.

The Tibetans say that when we die we have only one opportunity of merging into the Light, if we recognise the Light. If we don't, then we are bound to be reincarnated and live through this all over again. And to recognise the Light I imagine we have to get really accustomed to it.

During his last days Douglas kept telling me this. Some people asked him, 'What are you doing in your armchair, looking at the field?' He said, 'I'm getting used to being at home in the void.'

We drink our tea. After a while she says:

I'd like to add this: I just said that I am not afraid of dying, but I cannot know how I will feel at the moment of dying. When I really am dying, I might be afraid, like everyone, I cannot be sure. For the time being I trust.

I am not afraid because I think what is waiting for me on the other side is what I can see here when I see who I am. So it can't be bad. But it's still my belief. When I am really experiencing it I don't know if I will be able to say the same thing. Maybe I will be in fear and trembling.

I hope that I will remember Douglas' last words. He told

me to 'trust trust trust'. That was his motto, 'trust trust trust'. I'll try to remember this at the minute of dying.

'What exactly were Douglas' last words?'

His last words for me were 'I love you supremely'. And before that he repeated several times 'trust trust trust' when he saw that I was so sad. Then he said, 'Let me go.'

I've heard many people say that when their friends or their wife or husband or children are so sad when they are dying, it prevents them going. I should have known better, because I knew that. I shouldn't have been crying but I couldn't stop.

Now I often think of this, because I myself am entering into this process of getting old and having to let go of many things. I'm afraid that I was not always kind enough to Douglas when he was at the very end. It was so difficult to look after him. I remember having been impatient sometimes. And now I think, 'Oh, I was not really what I should have been.'

But maybe he did not feel it because he was already very low; maybe he did not realise it when I was impatient. I hope so.

'I think you were wonderfully patient, Catherine. I think Douglas knew you loved him supremely too.'

Oh, he knew that, of course. He could not have not known.

Epilogue

The next day Catherine's son drives me to the airport. She insists on coming along to wave goodbye. At the parking lot we hug and kiss: right left right left 'bisou bisou', as is the custom here in the south of France. 'Remember,' she says, 'that I love you.'

I think of what she said a few days ago, that the only choice we really have is to love someone or not. I have witnessed that love in action, and so I believe that she really does.

Back at home, in the challenges of my own life, I will suddenly remember words she spoke. To know that someone else, another woman, has lived through all the highs and lows of life just a little ahead of me and has come out so brilliantly, makes a difference.

'À toujours, Catherine!' I say with a smile.

When I walk away I feel I've lived an entire lifetime during this week. And found a true friend.

I turn around once more.

We wave.

Addendum to the 2nd Edition

Dear reader

Sitting at my desk and re-reading the Appendix on the following pages, I am reminded of how I first encountered Douglas Harding's work in a non-dual magazine published in The Netherlands called *InZicht*. Two weeks after finishing the first version of this book I was offered the position of chief editor of the same magazine.

Since becoming editor, I have been delighted to discover many more female voices across the globe. It has been my pleasure to introduce some of these women to the readers of *InZicht*.

Life moves in surprising ways. You may ask how did this happen? My suggestion is that you take the time to practice the following experiments as a way of surprising yourself.

Appendix – The experiments

I found Catherine's life story a fascinating and inspiring example of a woman's quest for the Light within. This is her story, though, and each of us has our own unique story. And so each of us will discover the Light within in our own way.

In my own case I've found the world a very strange place for as long as I can remember, and I was never able to make much sense of it. I kept asking myself, 'What is going on here? What is this life, this world? Where is my place in it and who am I?'

In my late twenties these questions became so acute that they led me on an inquiry from books to therapy, and from meditation to trips to India. In the meantime I had a career, got married and was blessed with two wonderful sons.

Then I met my first teacher (to whom I am ever grateful for his wisdom, sincerity and humour) and practised his teachings under his guidance until his death.

This method, however, did not fully satisfy my curiosity. I went through a divorce and kept looking for answers. I read more books, found another teacher and lived abroad in a spiritual community for seven years.

On my journey I met wonderful people and found important pieces of the puzzle, and I am deeply grateful for each of them. Yet even though so much had become clear to me, the total picture remained incomplete. What I longed for was to recognise beyond doubt and with absolute certainty who I was and where my place was in the universe. So I left the community and returned home.

The final missing piece – and the end of my quest – I would find almost three decades after it had started. Back in my home country I looked into what had been going on in terms of spirituality during my absence. I read some books, went to a few talks and flipped through non-duality magazines.

One day I read a short article in which Catherine Harding

talked about her late husband, Douglas. It was a loving and moving interview.

His name rang a bell. When I looked him up on the internet I found a website called *The Headless Way* (www.headless.org). It contained much of his philosophy and practices which he called 'experiments'. When I tried the first experiment I was blown away. I saw who I really was for the first time.

So what did I see?

I simple saw the full picture as it is here and now, and visible at every moment, if only we look.

The experiment itself was ridiculously easy and almost embarrassingly childish. I call it the ***See for Yourself experiment***. The tools are my own pointing finger and everything I see right now. Please join me and see for yourself.

> Point your finger towards an object some way away from you; it could be the wall of the room or a tree or hedge outside. What do you see? What is the colour of the object? What is its structure? Where are its borders?

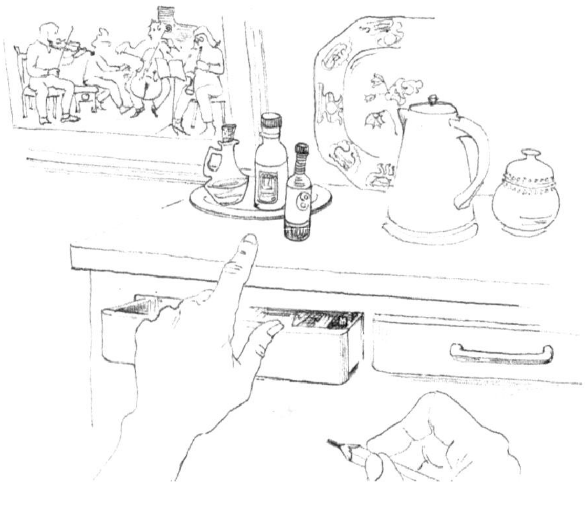

Now point at another object a little closer. Look, and answer the same questions. Point to something right in front of your feet and answer again. Point at your knee. What is its colour, its surface, its shape? Point at your belly, your chest, and answer again.

Take your finger up higher and point at your face. Look at your finger and answer the questions. Then turn your attention around and look at the place where others see your head. What do you see? Look without using your memory or making assumptions. Look as if you were a newborn baby who knows nothing about itself. What colour do you see here? What form do you see here? What structure do you see here? Do you see anything at all?

In my experience I see nothing; a spacious and borderless nothingness. The experience is direct and wordless and my mind doesn't know what to make of it.

You might say, 'I see nothing, so what's the big deal?'

But seeing this spacious emptiness here at my core is to me a deal beyond measure. And it is not empty: I see a headless body appearing from it and seamlessly extending into a world and a whole universe. In fact, I see my body and the world appearing *in* this spaciousness. In fact, everything I see *is* me.

The implications of this re-discovery are endless! They set straight all my learned ideas about myself and the so-called separate world. My misunderstandings about who I am and my place in the universe came from identifying with the wrong part. Here in the heart of it, I am not this limited person I see over there in the mirror; in the heart of it I am free of limitation. Here I am boundless and timeless. Here I am the One that contains Everything, right now and for ever.

I realised that nobody else could have answered my questions for me, simply because nobody else stands in my shoes or looks through my eyes. Nobody else has this exact viewpoint from here where I am. I had recognised the final answer to my inquiry, and I was the sole authority on that.

I think that the greatest contribution Douglas Harding has left to the world is his experiments. They make it possible not to have to rely on someone else's findings and testimonials, no matter how wonderfully and enchantingly they are described. The key is to see for yourself. It is a wordless and immediate experience.

Douglas' experiments showed Catherine how to see the Clear Light at will. You can have a look for yourself through the following experiment:

The Light within

Where is the Clear Light the Buddhists talk about? Let's have a look.

Hold out both your hands in front of you, pretending that they are glasses for your two eyes. Slowly pull your hand-glasses towards your face, so slowly that you can notice all the changing details along the way.

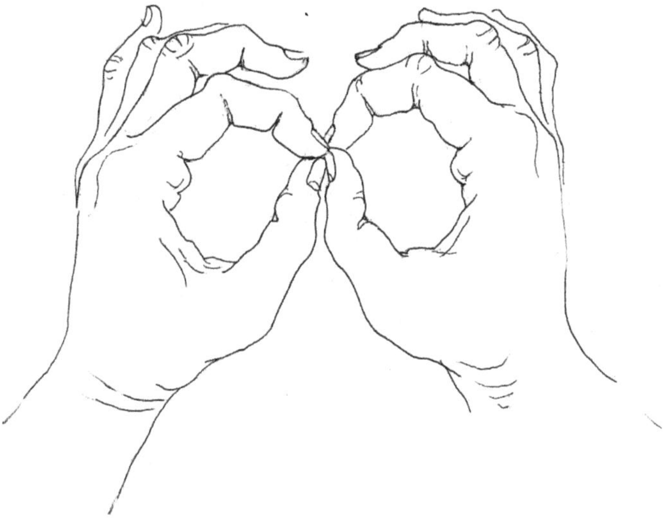

What do you see?

For me the contours of my hands become vague. The spot where my fingers touch in the middle becomes transparent and disappears almost completely. Finally my 'two glasses' merge into one field of vision.

Isn't this field borderless and limitless? And have I not looked out of this 'one eye' my whole life?

Whatever appears in it is brought to Light, the Light of my awareness. Isn't this what I am, the Light in which the whole world appears?

Even though I am this Light at heart, others address me constantly as a woman with a head. It is true: to them I have a head and a face. So where is this face of mine that I cannot see myself, for which I need a mirror, or a camera, or someone else's description?

Where is my face?

> Get a mirror and look at your face in the mirror. What is actually happening? Beside the fact that the mirror shows me what my face looks like, it also shows me where my face is – out there, framed by the mirror and at about an arm's length away. Here, above my chest, I find nothing. So who am I? That reflection over there? Or the space in which mirror and reflection appear?

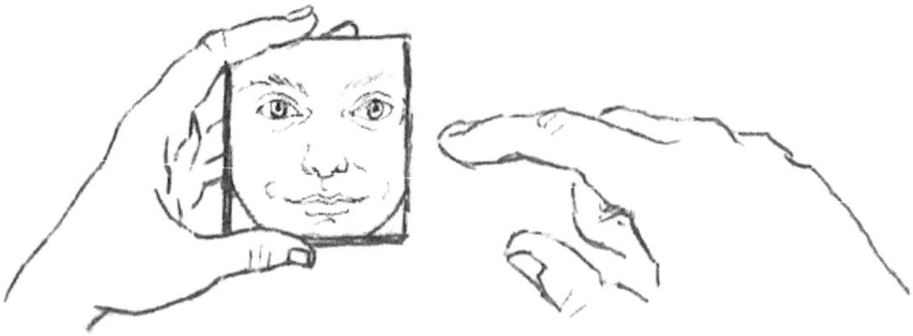

When I touch my cheek in the space here I feel a sensation. When I touch my cheek there in the mirror I touch a cold flat surface. Are these experiences in any way comparable?

So in reality I have two identities. For myself I am this spacious emptiness here at Centre, and for others I am a woman with a face, a face that I can see over there in the mirror. How do these two identities relate to one another? How does form relate to the formless? To investigate this you can do the following experiment, one of the main experiments in Douglas' workshops.

The Card experiment

> Cut out from a piece of paper an oval hole approximately the size of your head and hold it in front of you.

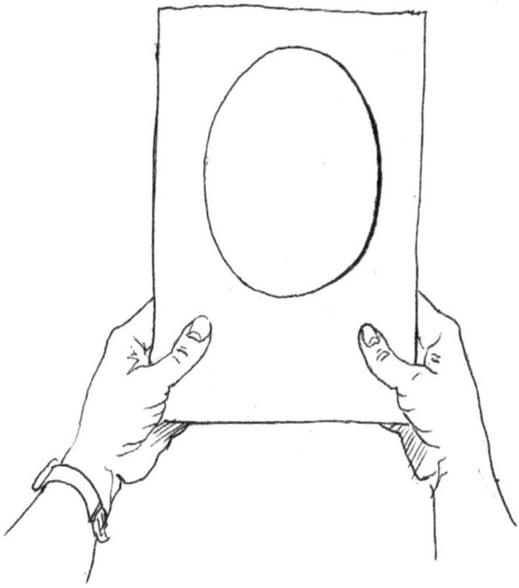

Look at the hole: isn't it small and limited? Isn't it void of anything and therefore spotless and perfect? Does it have anything to register time with? Do you see awareness there?

Now look at everything that appears in the hole: the colours, the shapes, the forms. Can you separate the space from what appears in it?

Pull the paper slowly towards you until the hole fits your face. What happens?

When I do this, I notice that the space gradually grows bigger, the edges get more vague and disappear altogether as the hole reaches my face. For me the emptiness explodes into a borderless immensity. Isn't the emptiness still perfect, spotless and timeless? But is it still unaware? I have become the aware boundless space. I have nothing of myself to keep the world out; I am the boundless capacity for the whole world to arise in.

Living in the world of form has led us to often believe that we are a form among other forms. In other words, that we are separate from everyone else and separate from our environment. This belief often creates a tension between ourselves and the so-called separate world. A way to embrace what is happening right now, no matter how it appears to you, is the following experiment.

A quick way back to who you really are

One of the quickest ways to get back to who we really are is just to have a look and see what your arms are coming out of. Your hands and arms are coming out of the big space that you are. It is not your little separate person operating these arms, the person you see in the mirror: rather is it the big One who you really really are who is moving these arms. You may find that everything is easier to do when you don't contract into your little one.

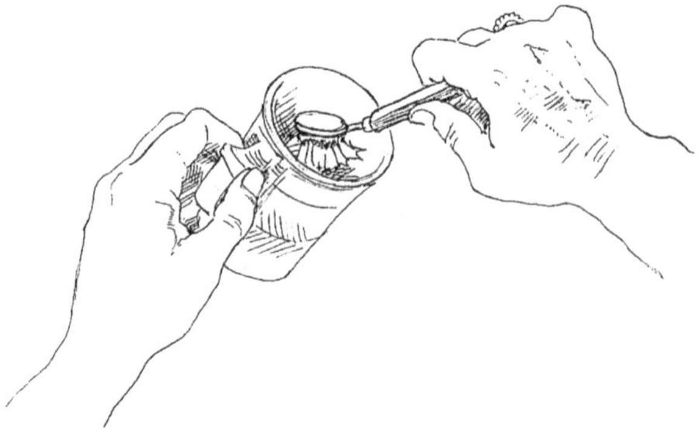

Although this experiment may not always work, and may not work for everyone, it's worth giving it a try.

Often we feel as if we are living in an unfriendly, if not hostile, world. Life is stressful. To have a body is stressful. In those moments when we believe that our body is a closed-off container, holding stress and contraction, the following experiment might help.

Bringing stress home

When you are in a stressful situation you can feel locked up in your body. Especially around your neck and shoulders tension can accumulate. An automatic response may be to push tension or pressure away from you, further outwards – which usually doesn't help. Here is an experiment to try in stressful situations:

> Bring your attention to the sensations of pressure in your body. Start by scanning the feelings in your feet, your legs, your body, your hands and arms. Where is the sense of contraction located?

Then bring your attention to the place around your shoulders where you see your body disappearing into no-thing, into the limitless space that you are here at Centre. Allow the knots of stress to cross that line with your awareness, and notice the effect it may have on your body.

In the space that you really really are appears the whole world, including all the sensations of stress and contraction.

Again, you may find that everything becomes easier to do when you don't contract into your limited self.

Most stress comes from interacting with others, and this closing experiment is Douglas' final word on the matter. Although the experiment is designed to be done with two people, you can also easily do it alone. When I did it for the first time there was nobody around except a statue of a woman: that served as my partner in the experiment.

The Tube experiment

You need some kind of a tube for this experiment, such as a paper bag with the bottom cut off that fits your face. As a partner you can use another person or, as I did, a statue of the right size, or your own reflection in the bathroom mirror.

> Fit your face into one end and place the other end against your partner's or the statue's face, or against the mirror.
>
> Now, going by what you actually see and not by what you remember or imagine: how many faces do you see in the tube? Is your end of the tube closed or open? Are you face to face with your own reflection or with the other face? Or is it a 'space to face' situation?

> When you put the tube down, ask yourself: has anything essentially changed? Do you still actually see only one face, the face there in front of you? Have you ever really been face to face with another face, whether it be a statue or a real person? Isn't there really always only the other face when you meet someone else? Can you see any separation between the space that you are here and the face over there? Isn't it really One?

❂

I hope you will benefit from these experiments as much as I have over the many years I have performed and shared them. Repeating these experiments over time grounded me in reality. And every time I really looked, I joyfully discovered another aspect, the genius and wonder of it all taking my breath away. For me, to find a true and immediately verifiable perspective on what I am has often made me laugh out loud. In difficult times it has offered me a chance to relax.

Most of the books on spirituality I've come across on my journey have been by men, and one of my motivations in writing this book was to add a female voice. In the world of form I am a woman and my life experiences, thoughts and feelings will be coloured by that. Yet when I take a look here at my Centre, I can discover no sex, age, nationality or colour of skin. Here at heart we are without gender.

Some of my most inspiring memories of being with Catherine include her constant use of seeing who she was in any given situation – not just as a thought that she was 'headless', but as an observable fact that was clearly apparent.

To be alive is a marvellous and challenging adventure. Here at heart we are free and open. Recognising that we are One make loves possible – we are the freedom to Love.

Acknowledgements

Beyond all else, thank you, Catherine, for trusting me with your life story, and for overcoming the conviction that your story wouldn't be of much importance to other people.

And without the encouragement and help of my dear friend Judy Bruce, right from its initial conception, this book would never have seen the light of day.

Thank you, Sequoia Star, Megan van Dyke, Deb Ray, Tom Musliner, Doug Manley and Michael Grant, for your help in transcribing the initial recordings.

Thank you, Catherine and Julian Noyce for your encouragement and advice, and for all your help in bringing this book to publication. A special thanks to Rose Youd for your insightful editing. Many thanks also to Jane Adams, who immediately agreed to my request to create the illustrations for the Appendix.

Thanks to my close friends, Lida Licht and Angela Baldinger, who never stopped asking about the book and who read and commented upon the manuscript from an early stage.

Richard Lang, thank you for your support and for your relentless enthusiasm and commitment to spreading the Headless vision around the world.

And a special 'thank you' to Amaranatho, my dearest partner, who designed the cover and who supported me in countless other ways.

About the author

Karin Visser is the chief editor of the Dutch non-dual magazine *InZicht,* founder of The Headless Café, poet and workshop leader. In her mid-twenties she started to enquire into the big question in life. After a search through books, meditation and therapy she met Jeru Kabbal, founder of the Clarity Process. She became his long-term student and wrote *The Quest for Clarity* (published in English and in Dutch) at his request. Jeru trained her to lead Clarity retreats, which she did for many years across Europe.

She was inspired to live in a spiritual community in Canada for seven years. Increasingly realizing that this did not bring her any closer to the truth, she returned home to The Netherlands. Shortly afterwards, she came into contact with The Headless Way. She recognised in Harding's experiments a radical breakthrough for spiritual seekers, enabling them to see directly who they truly are. She now runs the online community known as The Headless Café and shares Seeing.

Karin gives workshops and talks at home in The Netherlands and abroad. You can contact her through her website: www.headlesscafe.info.

Current titles from
New Sarum Press

Real-World Nonduality; Various authors

The Ten Thousand Things; Robert Saltzman

The Joy of True Meditation; Jeff Foster

"What The..."; Darryl Bailey

Lightning Source UK Ltd.
Milton Keynes UK
UKHW010609280223
417780UK00005B/567

9 781999 353551